Francis Marion
The Swamp Fox of Snow's Island

REBECCA DUNAHOE

ISBN 978-1-64114-447-6 (Paperback)
ISBN 978-1-64114-448-3 (Digital)

Copyright © 2017 by Rebecca Dunahoe

All rights reserved. No part of this publication may be reproduced, distributed, or transmitted in any form or by any means, including photocopying, recording, or other electronic or mechanical methods without the prior written permission of the publisher. For permission requests, solicit the publisher via the address below.

Christian Faith Publishing, Inc.
296 Chestnut Street
Meadville, PA 16335
www.christianfaithpublishing.com

Printed in the United States of America

To my family of birth: my parents, Richard and Myrtle Hughes; brothers: Jack, Ned, Carroll, Arlet; my sisters: Mary Nell, Lydia Hughes.

To my family of choice: Bill Dunahoe, Eve Dunahoe Hayes, and Richard Dunahoe.

To all those who have given to me stories passed down from one generation to another by word of mouth, scraps of paper, and newspaper articles. As I searched the records in archives and history rooms, libraries, and vertical files, I found so much good information, but not all gave their sources.

Contents

Foreword 7
Acknowledgments 9

Explanations 11
Francis Marion: The Swamp Fox of Snow's Island's Ancestors 13
His Will 14
Some of the First Settlers 15
The Descendants 24
Church History 25
Shipwreck 27
Landowners of Snow's Island 29
Waterways 31
Indian Involvement 33
Witherspoon's Ferry 50
Patrick Henry, 1775 52
The Revolutionary War 53
The South Carolina Rangers 65
The Swamp Fox Earns His Name 94
The Sharpshooters 96
Wemyss's Foray and the Hanging of Adam Cusack 98
War-Torn South 113
Skirmish at Black Mingo Creek 123
Old Fort Watson 125
The Swamp Fox at Black Mingo Bridge 146
Halfway Swamp and Singleton's Mill 152
Race to Singleton's Mill 154
Parker's Ferry 160
Marion at Port's Ferry 168
Leonard Andrea 175

Foreword

For more years then I can remember, I've been interested in Francis Marion's *The Swamp Fox of Snow's Island*. I was raised about five miles from Snow's Lake, a small lake that comes off Moody Island and Snow's Island. I began in early 1980 and stored in boxes every scrap of material I could gather about my hero, Francis Marion.

When I retired, my husband, Bill W. Dunahoe, and I moved back to our hometown, Hemingway, South Carolina. I've been working on this material for over twenty years. Some of those years I spent researching to identify some of the stories in order to give credit. Some I located; others I did not. If I've inadvertently used other's work, please contact me so that I may make corrections. Some of the material comes from vertical files with no source of identification.

—RHD

Acknowledgments

I would like to thank the many persons who helped me in the preparation of this book, acknowledging that I alone am responsible for all errors or omissions. No book is the product of one's mind or one's efforts alone. Among these who merit my constant gratitude, admiration, and love and who should receive my most sincere and heartfelt appreciation are the following:

> Alysia Carrigan, the compiler, who has contributed long hours of research and typing
>
> Daniel Carrigan, Debbie Hughes, and Christine Hughes for contributing hours of typing
>
> Eve Dunahoe Hayes and Jeanette Steward, who contributed hours of editing
>
> Sherman Carmichael, who encouraged me to complete the work of Francis Marion,

The Swamp Fox of Snow's Island

    Much of this information was gathered from my brothers (Jack, Ned, Carroll, and Arlet Hughes) and also from my sisters, Lydia Wafford and Mary Milling. The hunters and fishermen also passed their stories from one generation to another. Most of my seventy first cousins were raised around Snow's Island. They still hunt, fish, and camp out in that area. They also get together for Saturday cookouts, which includes eating, playing cards, and reminiscing about the past.

It is impossible to produce a large volume such as this, without the presence of errors. Much effort was put forth to eliminate them as much as possible, but errors are of a human nature. Please forgive such errors. Feel free to send corrections to: Rebecca Hughes Dunahoe, 400 North Lafayette Street, Hemingway, South Carolina 29554.

Explanations

RHD - Author Rebecca Hughes Dunahoe

Colonist - any original settler or founder of a colony

Piazza - an arcaded and roofed gallery; that is, a veranda or porch

Militia – (*1a*) any military force; (*1b*) later any army composed of citizens rather than professional soldiers called up in a time of emergency. (2) in the US, all able-bodied citizens between eighteen and forty-five years old who are not already members of the regular armed forces constitute the organized militia, all others the unorganized militia. (3) any of various disaffected groups of citizens that are organized as to resemble an army and that oppose the authority of the federal government.

Whigs - in the American Revolution, a person who opposed a continued allegiance to Great Britain and supported the revolution

Loyalist - in the American Revolution, a colonist who is loyal to the British government

Brigade - a large group of soldiers

Garrison - Troops stationed in a fort or fortified place

Tory/Tories - in the American Revolution, a person who advocated or actively supported continued allegiance to the British government

Redcoats - A British soldier in uniform with a red coat as to the American Revolution

Periauger - a large boat

Redoubt - a stronghold within a fortification

Ranger - a keeper, guardian, or soldier who ranges over a region (generally of wilderness) to protect the area or enforce the law

Dragoons - a member of any of several cavalry regiments in the British army

Francis Marion: The Swamp Fox of Snow's Island's Ancestors

Francis Marion's grandfather, Gabriel Marion, had fled the cruel persecutions of Louis XIV. Gabriel Marion and his family belonged to the sect of religious dissenters that bore the name of Huguenots (a supporter of any protestant in reference to the Calvinist Reform; any French protestant of the sixteenth or seventeenth century). They fled France and were received by England. They left England to come to the new world of America about twenty years after the first settlement of Britain in the province of South Carolina. They settled along Santee River about forty miles north of Charleston and about twenty miles south of what is now the seaport of Georgetown. Take a look in the early history of the Swamp Fox. His grandparents, Gabriel and Louisa, left their countries, France and England, for the sake of their religious freedom. His will shows him free. He appears to have been of a cheerful sort, not with gloom, but a happy Christian with a heart of joy.

His Will

I bequeath "my soul to God who gave it," and "my body back to the Earth in which it was taken." In the first place, as to debts, thank God, I owe none. And therefore shall I give my executors but little trouble on that score. Secondly, as to the poor, I have always treated them as my brethren. My dear family will, I know, follow my example. Thirdly, as to the wealth with which God has been pleased to bless me and dear Louisa and children, lovingly we have labored together for it, lovingly we have enjoyed it – and now, with a glad and grateful heart, do I leave it among them.

I give liberally to my children; but far more to my wife. I give my ever-beloved wife, Louisa, all my ready money that she may never be alarmed at a sudden call. I give her all my fat calves and lambs, my pigs, and poultry that she may always keep a good table. I give her my new carriage and horses that she may visit her friends in comfort. I give her my family Bible that she may live above the ill tempers and sorrows in life.

Marion Gabriel's oldest son was also named Gabriel. He married Miss Charlotte Cordes of French extraction. They had six children—Gabriel, Esther, Isaac, Benjamin, Job, and Marion. Marion's Gabriel's son, Gabriel, was the father of Francis Marion. Francis Marion was born on January 22, 1732.

When Marion was six, the family moved from his birthplace in St. John's Parish to a modest plantation on the banks of Winyah Bay near Georgetown. His father died when Marion was about eighteen. As the only unmarried son, he remained home with his widowed mother and took charge of the family plantation. He stayed in the rice country of Georgetown for the next five years. He then moved with two of his brothers back to St. John's Parish.

Some of the First Settlers

On the banks of Black River flowing ceaselessly beside us today, the first struggling white settlement began life around the King's Tree in Williamsburg Township two hundred years ago.

In 1729, the Lord's proprietors of Carolina were forced to relinquish the deed to the province given them by Charles II, and seven-eighths of the present state of South Carolina was bought by the Crown for less than $120,000. The Lord's proprietors had failed to make the province a growing and prosperous one. Only Charleston and Beaufort were permanent settlements, besides a few scattered homes in the coastal region. England realized that if Carolina was to be self-protecting from Indian and Spanish raids and valuable to the crown because of exports, the backcountry must also be populated. Therefore, in 1730, Governor Johnson was directed by His Majesty to lay out eleven townships on the navigable rivers: two on the Wateree, one on the Black, and one on the Waccamaw. Each township was to consist of twenty thousand acres, with a site for a town on the banks of the river. Each original settler was given fifty acres granted by the king.

Long before the survey of these townships, an unknown explorer returned to Charleston with the tale of a great white or short leaf pine that he had discovered in his canoe trip up the Wee Nee (Black) River. Since the tree, he said, was like those that grew in the north that were, with gold and silver mines, reserved in grants of land for use by the king as ship masts in his sailing vessels, the discoverer had marked it with a broad arrow, as all the King's Tree country with its primeval forests and endless swamps spread beyond Charleston and to the whole country.

Lured by tales of this land, two Charlestonians, Rutledge and Finlay, penetrated across the Santee through what is today Williamsburg County where two bays yet bear their names. Canals and ditches still faintly discernible attest that here the culture of rice was attempted and abandoned, thus ending the first attempt at settling the King's Tree region. Covered with a luxuriant growth of trees and vines, these bays begin four miles below the present town of Kingstree and extend to what is now Cades. The waters of Finlay Bay course into Board Swamp, while the waters of Rutledge Bay are the principal source of Lake Swamp, from which Lake City takes its name.

Of this fertile, undisturbed region, harassed Presbyterians, driven by persecution from their homes in Scotland to County Down and Ireland, heard longingly. Upon their petition that was the Wee Nee Township that was given them, they were furnished passage in 1732. Leaving behind them all that was familiar in life, this little band of forty set forth upon the broad Atlantic to find their new home in the wilderness. In this first colony were the families of Roger Gordon, who was leader of the band; Edward Plowden; Robert Ervin; James Armstrong; David Johnson; Adam McDonald; William James; Archibald Hamilton; David Wilson; and John Scott.

Their boat landed in Charleston whence they sailed up the coast to Winyah Bay. There they entered the mouth of Black River and followed its dark, winding waters to what is now Brown's Ferry, where they disembarked. From there to the dry lands on which stood the King's Tree was a journey of some forty miles. No sign of human habitation met their eyes; no sound of human voice fell on their ears. A stillness of the primitive, fathomless silence surrounded them, broken only by the song of birds unknown to them or the harsh cry of a wild animal. Strange gray moss hung from the unfamiliar trees and clouded the atmosphere as if with lavender haze.

The only recorded incident of their heroic journey comes down through the descendants of David Wilson in whose family the story was told of how the aged members of the band and the children were left to bring up the rear on the long trek from the landing place to the King's Tree. Sometimes those at the head of the forlorn procession were lost to sight in the dense forest, behind whose towering trees dreaded Indian savages might lurk. Terrified whoops would come from the rear stragglers, "Oh-hoo! Where are you?" And the heartening voices in their Scot-Irish brogue would call back, "Follow the blazes!" So each tree of the forest must be searched for the axe blaze that marked the way.

When they arrived in King's Tree, branches were hastily cut and stacked in rude huts covered with wet sand by the brave settlers to protect their women and children that first night from venomous serpents, prowling beasts, and the noiseless approach of Red Men.

Thus began the first settlement around the King's Tree. The township was named Williamsburg by request of William James, in honor of William of Orange, the Presbyterian king who came from Holland to ascend the English throne. Under him, John James, father of William, had fought in the wars in Ireland. John James left his home in Wales at the age of sixteen on account of a dispute with his sovereign over the contents of a fish pond. He joined Prince William's army as a cadet and rose to a captain of the dragoons. He never returned to Wales to claim the barony that was left to him, preferring honor to riches. After the wars, John James settled at Drosmore, County Down, in Ireland, and his two sons, William and John James of the lake, settled in Williamsburg.

In 1734, the first struggling settling was augmented by the Witherspoon colony under the leadership of John Witherspoon, the patriarch, who sailed on the ship *Good Intent*. John Witherspoon and his wife, Janet, had seven children who settled in Williamsburg. Elizabeth (the wife of William James) and Mary (the wife of David Wilson) had preceded their parents with the first colony.

The Witherspoon, like most of Williamsburg's early settlers, were Scots-Irish and traced their ancestry back through Margaret Stuart, second wife of John Knox, to Robert Bruce. The so-called Scots-Irish people, who came originally from Scotland and settled in counties Down and Antrim in Ireland on account of religious persecution, are traced back to the days before Christ. Their ancestors were the first settlers of Ireland and Scotland, except for the half-savage Pacts. Because of countries of religious wars, they had been herded together in two Irish counties from which they emigrated to America and were known as "Poor Protestants." But among the early settlers of Williamsburg, there were many whose forebears had been deprived of wealth but whose lineage was second to none in nobility. Among those whose distinguished coats of arms are well-known are the Scotts, the Witherspoons, the Nesmiths, and the Greggs. In the private annals of many other Williamsburg families, there are doubtless records of ancestry, also a proud heritage.

These "Poor Protestants" who founded the county in which we live in today sought this country as a refuge. Freedom to live in peace without interference and freedom to worship God as their hearts dictated beckoned them to Williamsburg. Out of such colonies, America became the land of the free and chose as its national creed only the solemn words "In God we trust."

Of the sailing of the Witherspoon Colony in 1734, a graphic account was written by Robert Witherspoon, grandson of John and Janet, and this narrative has been incorporated in several histories. The party was sent on from Charleston just after Christmas in an open boat, and after the immigrants disembarked at Potato Ferry, the boat continued upriver to the King's Tree with food and stores and was believed to be the first white man's boat that had ascended the streams so far. A year's provisions (consisting of Indian corn, rice, wheat, flour, beef, pork, rum, and salt) were given to each settler, besides a cow and calf for every two families. Horses were also brought, and for every hand over sixteen, an axe was allowed as well as one broad and narrow hoe. The weaker members of the party remained in Samuel Commander's barn while the men went on with a few horses to prepare dirt huts, or potato houses, for their families.

"As the woods were full of water and the weather was very cold, it made it go very hard with the women and children," says the record of Robert Witherspoon. It continues, "The next day every one made the best they could to his own place. This was on the first of February 1735, when we came to the place called the bluff, three miles below the King's Tree. My mother and we children were still in expectations of coming to an agreeable place, but when we arrived and saw nothing but a wilderness, and instead of a comfortable house, no other than one of dirt, our spirits sank; and what added to our trouble was the pilot who came with us from Uncle William James's left us as soon as he came in sight of the place. My father gave us all the comfort he could by telling us that we would soon get that we should be able to see from house to house.

"While we were here, the fire went out that we had brought from Boggy Swamp. My father had heard that up the river swamp was the King's Tree. Although there was no path, nor did he know of the distance, he followed up the meanderings of the swamp until he came to the branch and by that means he found Roger Gordon's place. We watched him as far as the trees would let us see and returned to our dolorous hut, expecting never to see him or any human being any more. But after some time, he returned with fire and we were somewhat comforted, but evening coming on, the wolves began to howl on all sides. We then feared being devoured by wild beast, and we had neither gun nor dog, nor even a door to our house, howbeit we set to and gathered fuel and made a good fire and so we passed the first night.

"The next morning being clear and moderate, we began to stir about, and about midday came a cloud from the southwest, attended with high wind, lighting and thunder. The rain quickly penetrated through the poles of the hut and brought down the sand with which it was covered and which seemed for awhile to cover us alive. I believe we all sincerely wished to be again in Belfast... We had a great deal of trouble and hardship in our first settling, but the few oppressed with fears on divers other accounts, especially being massacred by the Indians, or bit by snakes, or torn by wild beast, or being lost and perishing in the woods, of whom there were three persons who were never found...Another circumstance which gave us great alarm was the Indians when they came to hunt in the spring. They came in great numbers like the Egyptian locusts but were never hurtful."

Encouraged by the success of their Herculean labors in hewing homes out of the forest and snatching farm acres from the wilderness, this God-fearing band of settlers soon longed for a church where they might go to worship and a pastor from their own Church of Scotland to guide them. Gavin Witherspoon, son of John, met some of his neighbors and in his half-Scots, half-Irish brogue said, "Wull, we must have a minister."

So William James was chosen in 1737 to present a petition from the Williamsburg colony for land on which to build their church, and the Rev. Mr. Wilson of Dundee was called as the first pastor. In his stead came the Rev. Mr. Robert Heron, and under his ministry, the Williamsburg Presbyterian Church prospered. For some reason, the petition for a church plot was not granted until 1741, and in the meantime, land had been purchased from Roger Gordon and the first edifice of logs erected in August 1736 on the site of the Williamsburg cemetery today. John Witherspoon, who died three years after settling in this communityc was the first person buried in the graveyard.

The list of early settlers of Williamsburg Township read almost like the county record today since the same names continue prominent in local affairs. It must be remembered that the township had not the same boundaries as the present county. Part of the present county that lies adjacent to the Georgetown County line was then known as Winyah and was settled before King's Tree. The Rev. William Screven, South Carolina's first Baptist minister, settled in Winyah as early as early as 1710 with a colony of dissenters from the Church of England, who were largely Presbyterian in faith. Samuel Commander in whose barn the women of these early settlers stayed.

Slowly the clay huts and log cabins of the Irish colony multiplied and were gradually replaced by better homes. The woods yielded plentiful game; the dark streams and lakes abounded in succulent fish for the tables. Though they were able to work a living from the soil and from their increased herbs, overworked and low country disease, for which they were unprepared, perseverance and industry was by degrees rewarded. The bounty of the Crown assisted them until they made a living from the soil and their increasing herbs of cattle and hogs, which fattened on the rich pasture lands. They raised sheep; they grew flax, and there were weavers among them to make linen and garments for their needs. There were reed makers too who added to their household furniture and tanners who converted hides into shoes, coats, chair bottoms, and even into what served as bedsprings stretched between four posts. After some years, they were allowed the importation of a few slaves. The Negro race, accustomed to a hot climate and savage conditions, assured the successful settling of the South by the white people. Dark as many see the bolt of slavery, it appears in the light of our early history as an instance of the mysterious way God works His wonders to perform.

Besides the Scots-Irish, the Huguenots played an important part in Williamsburg's history. Holding the same faith as the Scots-Irish, the Huguenots were like them—driven from France by religious persecution and migrating to America. They settled in Charleston and in the back country along the Santee, and before 1737, made their way across the river at Lenud's Ferry into Williamsburg. The French names in this community, such as Gourdin, Lesesne, Mouzon, Mishoe, Prevatte and others, have come down from the Huguenot settlers who intermarried with the Scots-Irish.

Such was Williamsburg colony with the village of King's Tree as its vantage point.

And the women of Williamsburg—those first farm women who never met in council as we do today—we cannot pass in silence their courage and endurance. Had it not been for the women who bore for the sake of their faith the hardships of that early settlement in the desolate forest, we should not be here today. Picture them as they mastered their fear of beast and savage in this wild land. Picture them hiding their tears of loneliness from their menfolk and from their frightened children who clung round their skirts. Think of your comfortable homes and envision them in their humble dwellings with only the rudest implements for their household tasks as they went quietly about the creation of their homes. Marriage and birth and death—the trinity of human experience—came to those women of Williamsburg, who met pain and grief and happiness with a light in their eyes, a smile on their lips, and a prayer in their hearts.

Some of the first settlers in Craven County on Black River were twenty-seven indentured persons brought in by a man named James Gordon in 1734. Each settler was given eight bushels of corn and a peck of salt. In 1731, Meredith Hughes of Craven County was given a grant of over five thousand acres in Craven County. William

Clark received a grant of 450 acres beside the stream now known as Clark's Creek. Later in 1758, the Johnsons on Snow's Island, Andrew Johnson received 321 acres, and Archibald Johnson bought 560 acres of the Beal land and 300 acres from the heirs of James Gordon. Archibald Johnson willed his land to his son, Andrew Johnson, who then became the largest landowner on what was then called "Johnson Island." Eventually, Francis Goddard, a son of the merchant Francis Goddard, who lived in Charleston, bought the Johnson land.

While the island, later known as Snow's Island, was being divided by grants, a larger settlement was beginning across the Pee Dee River. Six Britton brothers received large grants in what is now known as Britton's Neck. "Britton's Neck is the tongue of land in Marion County that extends some twenty-five miles to the confluence of Pee Dee River and Little Pee Dee River. It was named for the Britten brothers Daniel, Francis, Joseph, Moses, and Timothy, who in 1735 to 1737 settled on a succession of sand ridges in projected Queensborough Township. Queensborough failed to form, but the Brittons, relatives, and friends built a flourishing community. " Phillip Britton and Timothy Britton married Jane Goddard and Mary Goddard, daughters of Francis Goddard. Their brothers, Francis and William Goddard, had followed their sisters to the island (Snow's Island) and settled there. William Goddard married a Britton sister, Elizabeth Britton, and they had a son that they named Francis Goddard. Then William Goddard died, and his widow married Samuel Jenkins. She became the "Widow Jenkins" who defied Colonel John Watson when he and his infantry camped around her home on March 7, 1781.

The brother, Francis Goddard, had married Ann Snow when he came to the island. Ann Snow was the daughter of Nathaniel Snow, a planter on Goose Creek. She was the granddaughter of Dr. Nathaniel Snow, a surgeon in Charleston. Francis Goddard and Ann Snow had a son they named William. Ann Snow's brothers, William and James Snow, became interested in Johnson's Island (later known as Snow's Island) after their sister and her husband moved there. William Snow received a grant of two hundred acres in March 1763. James Snow received a grant of a hundred acres in February 1768. Ann Snow

Goddard died about 1765, and her husband, Francis Goddard, died about 1777. When the earlier settlers began dying out, William and James Snow bought other tracts of land. William Goddard, son of Ann Snow and Francis Goddard, was about twenty years old when his parents died, and he was left with a lot of land. It was he who changed the name of the island to "Snow's Island" for his uncles who owned the most land.

The Descendants

William Johnson (1787–1851) was the son of Edward Drake Johnson and Amelia Owens of Muddy Creek. Their children were:

1. Nicholas Francis Johnson, who married Emily Snow, (1815–1891)
2. William Hill Johnson was a captain in the Confederate Army. He married Elizabeth Ann Woodberry, daughter of Brig. General William Woodberry and Elizabeth Johnson.
3. Margaret Ann Johnson (1823–1891) married Thomas R. Grier, son of James M. Grier and Elizabeth Covan of the Georgetown District.
4. James H. Johnson married Annie Pope and second, Clara Pope.
5. Sarah Johnson married Evander Woodberry, son of Brig. General William Woodberry and Elizabeth J. Johnson. Sara and Evander Woodberry died in 1870. A daughter, Olivia, became an early missionary to the Indians of Oklahoma.

Church History

As I look at my family's history, I find Captain Meredith Hughes, esquire, loyal to England his entire life. He helped start two churches, Prince George and Prince Frederick. Both churches were in Craven County under English rule and law. When some became uncomfortable with this, they began to move to Black Mingo Meeting House, or the Dissident Church, organized in 1726, located on Black Mingo Land, and was given in 1741 by William Thompson, Jr., to build a church building. Meredith Hughes stayed with the church at Prince Frederick and refused to leave its rules; if you lived in the church area, you paid taxes to that church. I often wondered what caused these settlers to cling to England and pay the taxes but have no voice in running their lives. It appears that William Hughes, son of Meredith Hughes, began to question England in the years just before the 1750s. By 1760, Charles Woodmason had established a store near Mingo, following a 1745 act by the general assembly that provided for clearing of the water courses at the head of Black Mingo Creek.

In 1706, the Anglican Church was established, and the colony divided into ten parishes. As they were under English rule, so were these parishes. In each parish, a church was to be built and a minister to be provided, and a register of births, christenings, marriages, and burials was to be kept. The people of the parish would elect assemblymen, church wardens, vestrymen, and overseers of the poor. Until the adoption of the US Constitution in 1789, the colonists were forced by law to support the Church of England. The Church Act, under the rule of England, established the parish of Prince George Winyah at Georgetown in 1722. Bounded on the southwest by the

Santee River and on the northeast by the Cape Fear River, on the east by the Atlantic Ocean and on the west as far as it shall be inhabited by his Majesty's subjects.

Shipwreck

At age fifteen, Francis Marion's family had moved to Georgetown, near the sea, and they probably spent time listening to sailors' tales of exotic lands and adventure. In those times, a long voyage at sea was thought to improve the health of sickly people. The Bahamas, Barbados, or Bermuda were all likely destinations for a voyage from Georgetown.

In his sixteenth year, Francis Marion decided to go to sea, probably against his mother's wishes. His slight build and small size made him an unlikely sailor, but he found employment on a small schooner bound for the West Indies. Six other seamen made up the crew. The name of the captain and the name of the ship are lost in time.

One account of the voyage states that the small ship was rammed by a whale or a swordfish and sank quickly. Most accounts say that the ship sailed into a terrible West Indian hurricane. Whatever the truth, the ship apparently sank with little warning, allowing the crew to escape in a little jolly boat (lifeboat). There was no time to load water or provisions. A dog from the ship swam to the small boat and was taken aboard by the seven sailors.

For two days, the jolly boat rode the waves of the mighty Atlantic Ocean. Her occupants must have suffered greatly from exposure, thirst, and hunger. Two sailors went mad and jumped into the sea and were lost forever. The remaining sailors killed the dog, ate his flesh, and drank his blood.

On the third day, the sea calmed and remained placid for another three days. By the sixth day, four of the five survivors were unconscious. Francis Marion was conscious but disoriented. At this critical point, when all were close to death, a passing ship sighted the little jolly boat and sent a party to investigate. Francis Marion was revived by his rescuers as were the other sailors in the little boat (although at least one account says that the other sailors did not survive). By the time Marion returned to Georgetown, he was much stronger, more robust, and better fit than when he left. He had also firmly resolved to not become a seafaring man and was content to farm with his family.

Landowners of Snow's Island

Gavin Witherspoon, son of Gavin, was born in Ireland about 1712 and came to America with the first contingent of relatives and friends. He married his first cousin Janet Wilson who died without issues and second Jane James, daughter of John James of Ox Swamp. Gavin Witherspoon died in 1773 and his wife in 1774. Their children were:

1. Mary Witherspoon (1740–1752)
2. John Witherspoon (1742–1802) married Mary Conn. Their only child was Elizabeth, who became the second of David Rogerson Williams.
3. Robert Witherspoon (1745–1787) married Mary James; died without issue.
4. Gavin Witherspoon (1748–1833) married first Elizabeth Dick and second Mrs. E. Thompson.
5. Jane Witherspoon (1751–1788) married Col. John Ervin of Marion's Bridgard.
6. Elizabeth Witherspoon (1759–unknown] married Col. Hugh Ervin of Marion's Bridgard.

John, Robert and Gavin Witherspoon and their brothers-in-law John and Hugh Ervin served in the South Carolina Legislature.

Snow's Island, near Johnsonville was part of Craven County and was named after Lord Craven of England; On May 24, 1913, a charter was issued incorporating the town of Johnsonville. For many years, the Williamsburg County line was Lynches River. In 1921, Johnsonville became part of Florence County.

Snow's Island was under water as the ever-changing swampland that Marion and his men called home. Finally, it was the natural rendezvous for the militia of Indiantown, Snow's lake, Mingo, Britton's Neck, and Witherspoon's. Witherspoon's Ferry acquired that name about 1767 when Robert Witherspoon purchased two tracts of land from Robert Withers of Georgetown District. For an unknown period of time, it had been known as Lynches Creek Ferry. Robert Witherspoon lived near the ferry, served in Marion's brigade, furnished large quantities of supplies to the Revolutionary War cause, and died on his plantation in 1787. He had no children, and upon his death, his ferry lands passed to his brother, John, who was a captain in the famous brigade. He died at his plantation in 1802. His deathbed will reveal a deeply religious and charitable man. The previous states, "I always intended the profits ensuing from the ferry land to be dedicated to the encouraging and propagating the gospel, promoting religious and moral principles." To achieve those purposes, he bequeathed the ferry lands to Airwell Presbyterian Church on the Pee Dee.

Witherspoon's Ferry was especially strategic to Marion's movements during the Snow's Island phase of the American Revolution in South Carolina. Located a few miles above the island on Lynches Lake, Witherspoon's Ferry at that time (Craven County and Williamsburg County) was the site at which Marion accepted command of the militia. The ferry was also on the important post road that ran from Georgetown to Cheraw and was the scene of exchanges of gunfire with both Tories and British soldiers.

Waterways

The waterways in the low country were where most of the Indians lived. Kadapaw of Lynches (this is where the Swamp Fox hid) was so called by the Indian tribe of the same name who lived in the forest and adorned its banks. Another early name for Lynches River was "Sara" or "Cheraw," once again in recognition of the Indian tribes living in the area. As its waters continue their journey and the drainage of swamps like Cypress Creek and Lake Swamp contribute to their runoff, it gains in both depth and width. The water, when at stable level, is not black; nor is it muddy like the Great Pee Dee, but it takes on a unique brown with a hint of green. About ten miles before its junction with the Pee Dee, it is at its widest and deepest. A few miles below the site where John Witherspoon operated his ferry, years later the waters seem to become impatient to reach their destination and seek three different routes. The first is locally referred to as the "Cut," a narrow, shallow stream that moves twice as fast as the main body until it spreads out in Snow's Lake. At a mile or so past Sockee Swamp, these waters join the second outlet, Clark's Creek. Then they travel together the seven miles on the Pee Dee and then another sixty-three miles to meet the sea at Georgetown.

The Cut is also known as Lawrence Cut. Local folklore says it was dug by hand using slave labor. It is straight, and it dumps into Snow's Lake. The banks are high at the start, so water probably never flowed there before. Keep in mind that Lynches Creek has a natural log jam caused by the Pee Dee River that has always prevented boats from accessing the Pee Dee. Clark's Creek splits Moody and Snow's Island, beginning at the northern end of Snow's Island. Clark's Creek crooks a left hand turn just below Snow's Lake, thus causing all the confusion between the Lynches, the Cut, and Clark's Creek. Cut

Landing was always known as a good Indian village site. Snow's Island is a point of land in the southeastern corner of Florence County in South Carolina. It also is where Marion County and Georgetown County come together with Williamsburg County. It is surrounded by waters of the Pee Dee River, Lynches River, and Clark's Creek. The island is about four miles long and two miles wide. It has sandy ridges similar to the land around old Britton's Neck, which is nearby. The island lies in the old township of Queens Borough. Queens Borough Township was laid out on both sides of the Pee Dee River, where the Cheraw and Pee Dee Indians lived and hunted along the East Bank of the river. In 1682, it was deemed necessary to divide the inhabitants' parts of the province of South Carolina into three counties. Berkeley County embraced Charles Town and around the capitol, extending from Seaweed on the north to Stuno Creek on the south. Beyond this to the north was Craven County. To the south to Combahee River was Colleton County.

By 1760, Charles Woodmason had established a store near Mingo, following a 1745 act by the general assembly that provided for clearing of the water courses at the head of Black Mingo Creek. Soon thereafter, schooners began carrying local products outside the settlement. In the early 1760 Black Mingo settlement, later known as Wiltown, had developed on the creek. It was located about two miles from Prince Frederick Parish. Black Mingo later had a stage shop, tavern, and approximately twelve wooden houses in the late 1700s. The Spanish were the first white men to settle in the Carolinas. In the late 1600s, the English moved in along the coast near Charlestown and Georgetown, setting up trade with the Indians. A board of commissioners was appointed by the assembly to regulate this trade. William Waites, Sr., was chosen as factor and Meredith Hughes, Esq., as his assistant. They were to establish Indian trade to the north and a public store on the Black River to trade coats, blankets, shirts, knives, buttons, beads, tools, arms, ammunition, liquor, and rum for skins and furs.

Indian Involvement

British authorities organized the Grant Expedition of 1761 in response to hostilities with the Cherokee from the frontier of Virginia southward to the Carolinas. In South Carolina, Charlestown's citizens were anxious about Cherokee activities to the west. Some were itching to revenge frontier atrocities, so much so that words "scourging" and "chastising" became synonymous with attitudes toward the Cherokee. Those of Ninety-Six District, even closer to the Cherokee, lived in a state of terror for an Indian attack. Whether in Charlestown or Ninety-Six, talk of war provoked a sense of drama in the Carolina colony. Concerns took a number of concrete forms. Among those concerns were rumors of a Creek–Cherokee alliance, but that involved more than anything the imagination of the Carolinas. To the contrary, the Creek were enemies of the Cherokee.

Just as great a concern was the presence of Fort Toulouse, a French fort in present-day Alabama, and its influence among the Overhill Cherokee of present day eastern Tennessee. After all, Fort Toulouse was only seven days' march from Fort Loudoun and 425 miles from Charlestown. The fact that the French in the region had allied with the Creeks tended to irritate the British, yet it worked to the British advantage: The Creek dominance worked to limit Cherokee influence with the French.

Creek relations aside, some Overhill Cherokee did indeed look to the French for support and expected them to build a fort in their homeland. When the British expressed opposition to such efforts, the Cherokee pointed out that French lived among the British at Charlestown. It was not easy for British officials to explain that those French were Huguenots, coreligionists and loyal British subject.

Those Huguenots, of course, were the French who gave us Francis Marion.

Underlying all of this was the Indian trade, an often dishonest trade that served to alienate the Cherokee. That trade, coupled with land-hungry and ever-encroaching white settlement, led to misunderstandings, to hostilities and counter-hostilities, and to Indian-hating.

When Cherokee in South Carolina avenged atrocities against Cherokee in Virginia, the so-called Cherokee War escalated beyond measure. Add to this situation in the forts (Prince George in South Carolina and Loudoun in today's Tennessee), ostensibly built to control and protect the Cherokee. The immediate catalyst in South Carolina for war was the Cherokee murder of Lieutenant Coytmore outside Fort Prince George. The British retaliatory assassination of twenty-two Cherokee peace emissaries at the fort would only further escalate matters.

To the west, events at Fort Loudoun further fueled fears and war hysteria. The Cherokee took the isolated and vulnerable fort in August 1760 and slaughtered its captives. Afterwards, French authorities at Fort Toulouse sent out a boatload of men and supplies to take Fort Loudoun in the name of the French King. Although its crew negotiated the Mississippi and Ohio Rivers, they were unable to pass the "whirl and suck" on the Tennessee River at the site of present-day Chattanooga. The French did establish a trading post at the Chattanooga site, the same area where the war-faction Chickamauga Cherokee would settle in 1777.

With the frontier so volatile, talk of peace in Charlestown was unpopular, and Carolina was prepared to "humble the Cherokee" and "to bring them to their knees." The war, however, was unnecessary and Grant realized it. By the time Grant started his expedition, the French had fallen in Canada (the French and Indian War concluded), which had forced the Cherokee to look again to the British for supplies. Grant, however, had his orders from his superior. That superior, General Jeffrey Amherst, commander of British forced in North America, believed the fall of Fort Loudoun had disgraced the British army, and he wanted revenge. Cherokee hostilities at Fort Loudoun (and to some extent those at Fort Prince George) served much as a "Pearl Harbor" event for Carolinians and helped pave the road to war.

The Cherokee, by contrast, were ready for peace. Principal Chief Osconostota, who earlier had unsuccessfully sought French help in New Orleans, was now ready to talk peace. Following up, Cherokee peace-maker Little Carpenter (Attakullakulla) presented a peace overture before Grant had reached Fort Prince George, only weeks into his journey to the Appalachians. Grant, determined to carry out his orders, would not listen to Little Carpenter.

The ensuing war, termed the "Cherokee War" by the whites, consisted of three wars altogether: Governor Lyttleton's expedition (1759), the Montgomery Expedition (1760), and the Grant Expedition (1761). Marion and other young South Carolinians likely gained their first battle experience as part of the Montgomery Expedition, which ended in an ambush at Echoe Pass along the Little Tennessee River. Montgomery's army was not large enough to continue to Fort Loudoun and lift its siege as planned and had to return to Charlestown. The Cherokee continued raids on South Carolina settlements, its inhabitants irked that Montgomery had not finished the job. Charlestown area agriculturist Eliza Lucas Pinkney said that Montgomery had only "exasperated the Indians to more cruel revenge. What was been termed a Cherokee military victory over Montgomery was, in fact, a Cherokee political victory. Victory would not come until the final expedition, a full-scale assault under Highlander James Grant. A seasoned veteran of the Indian wars in Pennsylvania and second in command under Montgomery, he was familiar with Indian warfare.

Francis Marion enlisted on January 31, 1756, in the Indian war company of Upper St. John Parish. Although he marched as far west as Ninety-Six, he would not have participated in the Lyttleton Expedition; his company disbanded when Lyttleton concluded temporary peace with the Cherokee. Marion, therefore, would have first gained his experience in the 1760 Montgomery expedition. The late western North Carolina historian, Ora Blackmun, appeared to have had some insight when she referred to provincials as "seasoned regulars" under Grant. That Marion was an officer says something about his experience or leadership abilities.

It is in the final expedition that we first hear about Marion. He would have been aware that a number of South Carolinians had deserted out of fear of smallpox and measles. He would have been aware of the varied peoples on that expedition (from natives to the Royal Scots), and he would have experienced the danger and difficulties borne by Grant's army. He would have been aware of the friction between Grant and Middleton and between Grant and the entire cadre of Carolinians. He certainly came to know of Grant's Sherman-like march and the destructiveness wrought upon the Cherokee, expressed in a well-known letter.

The Grant Expedition got underway from Charlestown on March 20, 1761. Halting for three weeks at Moncks Corner for field-conditioning, it would increase in size as units joined in the Congarees on April 22 and at Ninety-Six on May 13. At full strength, it consisted of 2,828 officers and men, including two independent battalions (1,400), provincials (689), rangers (401), wagons (240), Indians (57), and African-Americans (81).

The Indian corps, under the command of Captain Quentin Kennedy, consisted of Mohawks, led by the noted Silverheels; Stockbridge Indians; Catawbas; Tuscaroras; and Chickasaws. King Haigler (Nopkehe) of the Catawba, known for his loyalty to the British, commanded twenty or more Catawba auxiliaries. James Adair, trader to the Chickasaw nation and author of *Adair's History of the American Indians* (1775), was also a member of the expedition. He had earlier recruited Savannah River and perhaps Charlestown-dwelling Chickasaws to serve with him as scouts under Montgomery and Grant. Included also was a regiment of Highlanders and a New England company of Major Robert Rogers' rangers, known for their Indian fighting.

Western North Carolina historian Ora Blackmun has placed North Carolina Colonel Hugh Waddell, a veteran of the investment of Fort Duquesne in Pennsylvania, with the Grant Expedition. In late 1759, Waddell assembled a force and marched to aid Lyttleton but concluded his march in January 1760 after he learned of a treaty between Lyttleton and the Cherokee. Later that year, Waddell and five hundred North Carolinas were instructed to assist Colonel William Byrd of Virginia in a diversionary expedition against the Cherokee to be coordinated with Montgomery's march from South Carolina. It is clear, however, that Waddell's North Carolinians and Byrd, himself, facing desertions and lacking adequate forces, had no heart for this campaign. Mustered into service again for seven months on May 1, 1761, Waddell and his North Carolinians could not have been with Byrd, who resigned earlier in the year. It appears, therefore, that they joined Grant's march, already underway. Waddell, who sometimes "dressed and acted as an Indian," could have been responsible for recruiting some of Grant's Catawba auxiliaries.

Most important to this study: A South Carolina provincial regiment commanded by Colonel Henry Middleton included William Moultrie, Henry Laurens, Andrew Williamson, and Francis Marion, all officers. Waxhaw's resident Andrew Pickens was part of the expedition as was Isaac Huger, a low country Huguenot. Both appeared to have been officers.

It was no doubt an impressive sight as the army moved west. Middleton's provincials, including Marion, joined the larger forced at the Congarees on April 22. On May 25 and 26, Chickasaw and Catawba reinforcements added to the total. At Fort Prince George, the army camped for eleven days. There, a Cherokee settlement adjacent to Fort Prince George.

By June 7, the army had moved beyond Fort Prince George and the remains of the Lower Settlements destroyed by Montgomery the previous year. Now forming a column at least two miles long, Grant's army began marching to the middle settlements of the Cherokee. In front and along the sides were the Indian corps who served as scouts. Next, as an advance guard, came the South Carolina rangers and British light infantry. Following, came the heavy battalions, including the Highlanders, followed by the provincials. Beyond was a six-hundred-horse packed train with baggage, ammunition, and flour, all guarded by rangers and light infantry. Bringing up the rear were cattle managed by cowboys and rangers.

The expedition's first great elevation gain was what its participants termed Oconee Mountain, located in present-day Oconee County, South Carolina. Much of that original trail is today incorporated into the Palmetto Trail section from Station Falls (Oconee Station Historic Site) to Oconee State Park. Beyond the mountain and following rolling upland, the trail continued to a ford on the Chattooga River, now known as Earl's ford of the Whetstone Community. West of the river, the trail continued along Chattooga River tributary Warwoman Creek to enter a place known as the Dividings, so-named because streams and trails were said to have led in many directions. From the Dividing (now the town of Clayton, Georiga), the trail turned north, passing today's Mountain City and the Tennessee Valley Divide, identified by a rise known early as the Passover. There, Warwoman Creek and other streams to the south flowed to the Chattooga drainage, to the Savannah and to the Atlantic. Just beyond, to the north, Wolf Fork Creek, Betty's Creek, Kelly's Creek and others formed the headwaters of the Gulf of Mexico. Beyond Rabun Gap and today's Dillard, Georgia, the valley would eventually widen to display rich savannah and river-cane bottomlands.

The widening bottomlands would not continue, however. As the expedition moved north along the Little Tennessee River valley, it could observe low ridges and hillocks reaching closer to the river's edge. The Narrows was, as the name implies, the narrowest of this landscape, forcing British expeditions between a hillock to the east and the Little Tennessee to the west. It was at this point the Cherokee had attacked the Montgomery Expedition, and it is in the same area that they also attacked Grant. The narrowed area became known as Echoes Pass, after the Cherokee village just to its north.

Grant did not want to repeat the mistake made by Montgomery. The Cherokee, however, saw it differently. They would turn back Grant as they had Montgomery, deploying on either flank and fighting at long range until Grant reached an open savanna, where they would attack his packhorses and force him to retire. Even before Grant reached the Narrows, the Cherokee waged psychological warfare, their scouts making themselves known to Grant's advance patrols. On a tree Grant's soldiers found a carving of a soldier being dragged away by two Indians.

As his army entered what has been described by early historians as a ravine or defile (the Narrows) the Cherokee opened fire from both flanks with shot and arrow. Grant deployed provincials and rangers, including Francis Marion, to dislodge Cherokee on the hillock to the east, and sent another company after the Cherokee across the river to the west. By this time, the pack train had entered the Narrows, and at once, the Cherokee attacked it and killed six rangers and drivers and up to sixty horses. Horses reared and kicked, raising a dust from the spilled sacks of flour and helping to make for a chaotic situation. The attack on the pack train could have doomed the expedition, but Grant was prepared. He sent back 175 provincials to rescue the pack train and drove his main force through the Narrow, his Catawbas fighting on the flanks and answering the yells of the Cherokee with their own.

Crossing Little Tennessee at Otter Ford, Grant pressed on toward the Middle Settlements, the second battle of Echo complete. He had not really won; he just made it through the Narrows and across the ford. The Cherokee retreated only because they had run out of powder and ammunition. It is easy to imagine that Cherokee rifle fire would have become less frequent, punctuated by more arrows at the end.

There is no doubt that Marion was involved at Echoes Pass.

William Willis Boddie in his *Traditions of the Swamp Fox: William W. Boddie's Francis Marion*, writes that Grant called for volunteers to dislodge the Indians from the summit of this hill and immediately Francis Marion and thirty of his men stepped to the front. Their ascents had to be made up a narrow defile upon which the Indians concentrated their position so that the army could advance, but twenty-one of that intrepid band of thirty-one had been killed. The leader of this fearless force had not even been wounded, although his clothing had been torn by bullets. Nearly three thousand colonial soldiers had seen young Marion and his men moving through that leaden hail, and since he had escaped injury, they thereafter regarded him as immune to fire.

Boddie's account of Marion's role is the most sensational and fantastic of any and makes Marion appear almost immortal. The author has documented his sources as Mason Locke Weems (*Life of Gen. Francis Marion*).

In fact, many of the firsthand and early accounts of the battle of Echo make mention of Marion's role. Perhaps it was Weems or Simms who concocted an expanded story to go along with the public notion of Marion as a Robin Hood who could make no mistakes. John P. Brown, in *Old Frontiers: The story of the Cherokee Indians from earliest times to the date of their removal to the west* (1838) lists no source when he writes simply that "Lieutenant Francis Marion with thirty Carolina rangers was sent ahead to explore the pass, closely followed by Captain Kennedy with ninety provincials and some friendly Indian scouts.

William Dobein James, who actually served in Marion's brigade in the American Revolution at age fifteen and published a sketch of Marion in 1821, writes with an air of authenticity about Marion at the Narrows:

In the same year, 1759, the Cherokee war broke out, and he turned out as a volunteer in his brother's troop of provincial cavalry. In 1761, he served in expedition under Col. Grant, as lieutenant in Captain Wm. Moultrie's company, forming part of a provincial regiment, commanded by Col. Middleton. It is believed that he distinguished himself in this expedition, in a severe conflict between Col. Grant and the Indians, near Etchoee, an Indian town; but, if he did so, the particulars have not been handed down to us by any official account. Grant Moultrie says of him, "He was an active, brave, and hardy soldier and an excellent partisan officer.

Hugh Rankin, in one of the most recent and best-documented biographies of Marion, *Francis Marion: The Swamp Fox*, (1974), throws documentation to the wind and waxes eloquent on Marion at Echos Pass:

The Cherokee had once again laid an ambush in a defile in which they had surprised Montgomerie. They had to be driven out before the army could advance. A detachment under Marion was given the task of clearing the pass. Cautiously the green lieutenant led his thirty men into the tangle of trees. The Indians waited until they were well within range before losing a blistering fire. Marion's advance was slowed as his men sought the protection of the trees. But even as the savages whooped, the lieutenant led his men forward, advancing from one tree to another. By the time they passed, twenty-one of his thirty men had been either killed or wounded.

Grant, during all of this, kept his army advancing during three or more hours of warfare, ending at around noon. About nine that evening, the army reached Echoe, which, along with the village of Tasse, they burned, and continued north along the trading path and the Little Tennessee bottomlands. It became routine: The Cherokee had fled each settlement; and Grant, with little opposition, destroyed crops, orchards, and dwellings, his Indian crops taking revenge on any of their traditional Cherokee enemies found straggling.

Taking possession of the deserted village of Nikwasi, Grant's army eventually moved on to other Middle Settlements, further north along the Little Tennessee. For three weeks, they destroyed crops and laid waste to the villages of Joree (Iotla), Watauga, Coweetchee, Burning Town, and Cowee. Again, few Cherokee were to be found; most had fled to the Cartoogechaye Creek and Deep Creek area of today's Macon and Swain counties respectively or to the Overhill Settlements of today's Tennessee.

As he had at Nikwasi, Grant used the mound and large council house at Cowee as a field hospital. Here too, at what was the largest of the Cherokee Middle Settlements, he cut his men's rations, determined to reach every town within marching distance. Leaving over a thousand provincials to protect the sick and wounded at Cowee, he led a detachment of 1,600 men across the Cowee range at night in a rainstorm in what became the most grueling march of their journey.

Taking this high mountain route to gain the element of surprise against the outlaying Cherokee, Grant's detachment followed Beasley and Huckleberry creeks and crossed the Cowees at Leatherman Gap (at an elevation of 4,300 feet). From there, they descended the trail along the headwaters of Alarka Creek and, following Connelly Creek, entered the Tuckaseegee River Valley and the outlaying settlements." Known by the British as the "Out Towns" the settlements were indeed remote. Regardless of their remoteness, Grant's mountain march was no surprise; the Cherokee learned his army was coming and again fled their villages.

For Grant, it was routine work. From June 16–28, his detachment went about their task of destroying the outlying settlements, including crops and winter stores. Among those villages were Stecoa and Kituhwa, the latter the Cherokee's most sacred town. Finally, returning to Cowee at a lower trail and west of the earlier mountain crossing, the detachment destroyed Tuckaleechee (at present-day Bryson City) and Tesuntee (unknown) on the way.

Destroying Cowee, as they had over villages, Grant and his army limped back to Fort Prince George on July 9. In all, Grant's army had destroyed fifteen middle towns and an estimated 1,500 acres of corn. According to anthropologist James Mooney, Grant had "pushed the frontier seventy miles farther to the west."

Grant would have wreaked further destruction, but his army was done in by the terrain. Veteran officers, referring to the Cowee crossing, agreed that "no such march was ever made by troops," likened by Grant as "much worse than the passage of the Alps," which he had claimed to have seen. As Captain Christopher French recorded in his diary, "The mountain, which is upward of two miles to the top and extremely steep which made a fatigue beyond description to get up it. [It was] the strongest country I ever saw, anything we had yet passed being nothing in comparison to it. [The] mountain...was so very steep and made slippery by the rain...that it was nearly difficult to get down as up." Grant's army, including "a thousand men...absolutely without shoes" were forced to turn back. It appears that, as an officer, Marion would have been part of the detachment across the Cowee Range.

But what of the Cherokee in all this? The numbers tell the story. in all, Grant drove some five thousand Cherokee men, women, and children out of their homes and into the mountains, where many starved. Anthropologist James Mooney recorded conditions among Cherokee:

"The Cherokee were now reduced to the greatest extremity. With some their best towns in ashes, their field and orchards wasted for two successive years, their ammunition nearly exhausted, many of their bravest warriors dead, their people fugitives in the mountains, hiding in caves and living like beasts upon roots or killing their horses for food, with the terrible scourge of smallpox adding to the miseries of starvation, and withal torn by factional differences which had existed from the very beginning of the war—it was impossible for even brave men to resist longer.

In the end, the Cherokee sued for peace, and according to the late Wofford College professor and historian Lewis P. Jones, "South Carolina seceded from the French and Indian War."

The French assistance that many had hoped for never materialized. With no strong ally, the Cherokee faced a national disaster brought on by a combination of events. Their resistance lowered by famine, many succumbed to smallpox epidemics. Cherokee historian Theda Perdue notes that, because of famine and epidemics, the Cherokee population was reduced to about one-half its prewar level. Moreover, lack of trade goods forced them to revert to ancient skills such as making clothes from animal skins and using bone as arrow points instead of brass. It was as if they returned to the Stone Age. As the loser in the war, the Cherokee would also surrender a great amount of territory.

They would never fully recover from the devastation inflicted by Grant and others. The late historian Chapman J. Milling (Red Carolinas) wrote that years after Grant's Expedition when Cherokee women found settlers' livestock trampling their crops, they would shoo the livestock away with cries of "Grant! Grant!"

Francis Marion saw the Indians march long distances, sleep on the ground, and fight for days without any food except a pouch of parched corn. He saw their war chiefs build their strategy around every feature of the land: every stream, swamp, thicket, wood, and hill. He saw them use their speed and mobility to surprise and disperse. And he learned that a small party can humble a more powerful enemy. In campaigning against the Cherokees in the Carolina phase of the French and Indian War, he learned strategy and tactics that would shake the British Empire, and shake it he did.

In the end, his solidarity with members of the low country gentry put Marion in good stead with Revolutionary authorities. The Cherokee War brought together the Carolina yeoman and rising planter class against a common enemy. That cooperation would be essential in the coming Revolution.

A great Indian road a distance of about eight hundred miles beginning first as Buffalo trail ran north and south through the Shenandoah Valley, extending from New York to the Caroline's still a part of Craven territory. The mountain ranges to the west of the valley are the Alleghenies, and the ones to the east constitute the Blue Ridge chain. The second Treaty of Albany (1722) guaranteed use of the valley trail to the Indians. At Salisbury, North Carolina, the great Warrior Path was joined by the Indians' "Great Trading Path." By the early 1740s, a road beginning in Philadelphia (sometimes referred to as the Lancaster Pike) connected the Pennsylvania communities of Lancaster, York, and Gettysburg. The road then continued on to Chambersburg and Greencastle and southward to Winchester. In 1744, the Indians agreed to relinquish the valley route. German, Scottish, and Irish immigrants had already been following the route into Virginia and on to South Carolina and Georgia. After 1750, the Piedmont areas of North Carolina and Georgia attracted new settlers. From Winchester to Roanoke the great Indian Wagon Road and the Great Valley Road was the same road; but at Roanoke, the Indian Wagon Road went through the Staunton Gap and on south to North Carolina and beyond, whereas the Valley Pike continued southwest to the Long Island of the Holston, now Kingsport. The Boone Trail from the Shallow Ford of Yadkin joined the road at the Long Island of Holston. The study of migration is particularly valuable to America, for all Americans are immigrants. Migratory people are profoundly mobile, moving from city to city and from state to state, as Alexis de Toqueville observed of early Americans, "The American grows accustomed to change." As the migrants moved, it was by the flow of water. It was much easier for them to travel.

And shake the British Empire he would. The Francis Marion of the Grant expedition was engaged in quite a journey, not as grueling as Arnold's expedition to Quebec or the battle on snowshoes, but grueling nonetheless. It was indeed Marion's field school. He was doing what was expected of low country gentry in his day. Not exactly a Robin Hood. Moody, introverted, not always popular, yet captured in the public imagination—this was Marion. It must be said that he used his training well. Of all those young Charlestown area men on the expedition, he perhaps learned better than any. It is not Gadsden or Middleton or Laurens that is the grand hero of the Revolution; it is Francis Marion, a soldier par excellence.

Note: All letters are recorded word for word as they were written. Letters from the Board of Indian Trade Commissioners (Tuesday, February 12, 1716–1717):

The board met by special summons. Those present were Col. George Logan, Ralph Izard, Esq., and Charles Hill, Esq. "William Waites, factor for Windaus (appearing) informs that he is just come down from the factory, having left the charge thereof with Mr. Hughes, his assistant, and that he hath brought down in the Periaugoe with him from thence, about six hundred skins on account of the trade, and about four score more, that Tom West, a PeeDee Indian (who comes in behalf of the Charraws to conciliate a peace with the government) bring with him to restore to those persons from whom the same was despoiled by the said Charraws upon the Revolt." The said Waites delivered a letter from Mr. Meredith Hughes, dated the 2d instant, as per bundle e (no 5) with an invoice from the said Hughes, of good wanting for the trade.

A letter from the board of Indian Trade Commissioners (Thursday, February 14, 1716–1717):

The board met according to adjournment. Those present were Col. George Logan, Ralph Izard, Esq., Col. Jno. Barnwell, and Capt. Jona Drake. Mr. Waties desired to be discharged of his factorship, and was answered by the board, that they do condescend to grant him leave to resign the same, but defer the cancelling of his bond until their next meeting, intending to settle and adjust all matters pending with him. He is hereby nominated and appointed principal Factor at the factory in Wineau, in room of Mr. William Waties, who hath declined that charge. Ordered that a fit person for an assistant to the said Hughes be provided in order to proceed in the Periaugoe with the goods and provisions intended for the factory at Wineau. Upon motion; ordered, that the storekeeper dispose of such Indian slaves, as he shall purchase of our friendly Indians, at Vandieu, as was before directed;in two days after they shall be so purchased, giving notice thereof, the day before; and that the clerk, do keep and render to this board, a particular account of such sales; and that every slave be sold singley, unless a woman with her child; and that the storekeeper be served with a copy of this order. Adjourned, till further summons.

In a letter to the Lord Proprietors in 1720, Governor Robert Johnson estimated the number of the various Georgetown and Williamsburg Indian tribes: Sarows (Cheraws): 510; Wacammaw (Waccamaws): 610; Santees and Congarees: 125; Seawees; 57 and Winiaus: 106.

Taken from *House of Hughes and Dunahoe and Their Many Relatives* by Rebecca Hughes Dunahoe:

James Wesley Hughes (Little Daddy), my grandfather, was a direct descendant of Meredith Hughes, the Indian Trader. It was from "Little Daddy" that we have the recipe for "pine bark stew"; it was handed down from one generation to another. His grandmother was an Indian, but I have not found the tribe to which she belonged.

The stew was called pine bark stew because it was cooked with pine bark that had no flame, so the enemy could not see the fire. Stack up the pine bark, start fire, put a large pot half-full of water over the smoothing bark. Gather what's available in rivers, swamps, and farms; meat such as squirrel, deer, fish, and cattle. Put in the pot dish (cat) or flat-cleaned. Or is there any other meat available? Add tomatoes (farm or wild), onions (white) or sweet potatoes, bay leaves (one or two), any vegetable found on the farm, okra, beans, corn, or any food in season. Boil until done. This stew was what the "Swamp Fox" used to feed his "fellows" as he kept his base on Snow's Island.

Our house had what he called a piazza or porch. Every evening in the summertime, we would sit around, and "Little Daddy" would tell us yarns passed down from his ancestors. In the wintertime, he would keep a fire going in our fireplace and we would all sit around the fire, and he would roast sweet potatoes and nuts, such as pecans, hickory nuts, and walnuts. He would also build bird traps and catch and clean the birds and put them on a clean stick, and we would roast them over an open fire. Little Daddy would store summer fruit in big oak barrels. He would take white sand sift it and then put a layer of pears, a layer of apples, and more sand until he would fill the barrels. He would close them and seal them, and we would have fruit for the winter from barrels in the smokehouse.

The story that was handed down even to this generation was of his grandfather taking the oxcart and going to Black Mingo Creek to pick up supplies for the trading posts. The oxcart could move easily through the trees because streams had to be forded, and there were no roads. As the paths were mostly trails to Smith's Mill the supplies come on a flat bed float with poles used to navigate the waters. He and his grandfather would leave early to meet the raft that brought supplies from Georgetown to Will Town, or Smith's Mill. They would then return with the supplies to Lambert later known as Hemingway.

By 1770, there probably were not more than ten thousand White settlers in the Pee Dee, but the edge had been taken off the wilderness. By that time there were more settlers and road trails. Substantial commerce flowed down the Pee Dee, Lynches, and Black River in the form of corn, animal skins, and indigo. Roads were sufficiently passable to allow cattle and wagons to be taken to Charles Towne. On Black Mingo Creek, near the present Highway 41, Will Town and Smith Mill little village's once thrived with stores, taverns, and several inns.

Francis Marion and his brother, Job, were elected to the Province Congress that assembled in 1775 to take into consideration the feeling of colonies toward the mother country.

After the French and Indian War ended in 1763, he resumed the planter's life and bought Pond Bluff Plantation on the Santee River near Eutaw Springs. There he prospered. In 1775, he was elected to the South Carolina Provincial Congress, which sent delegates to the Continental Congress meeting in Philadelphia. Later, when the dispute between the colonies and Britain turned into war, the Continental Congress called on South Carolina and the other newly formed state to provide troops for a national army. Marion was elected captain of the Second South Carolina Line.

Francis Marion, Humble Beginnings to a Great Adventure
When the British committed many injustices in 1775, they forced upon America the War of the Revolution.

Margaret Gorden:

She is counted one of the heroines of the Revolution. The following incidents are related of her in the Rev. James A. Wallace's *History of the Williamsburg Church*. "Pending the predatory warfare of Hamilton in Williamsburg, a party of marauding Tories went to the house of Captain William Gordon and commenced plundering the house. But conscience makes men cowards. The alarm was given, whether false or not, does not appear that the Whigs were coming when the whole party fled. One of them, becoming fastened some way in the fence, was unable to get over. Mrs. Gordon ran and caught the fellow and pulling him down on her side of the fence detained him until help came and he was secured."

"At another time, the freebooters came and carried off all Mr. Gordon's horses while he was absent fighting the battles of his country. Mrs. Gordon, unable to prevent the robbery, followed the party at a distance and observed where the horses were enclosed. That night she went alone, caught the best horse in the lot (better than any of her own) and, mounting him, rode away in safety with her reprisal."

Margaret learned of Cornwallis preparation to send Tarleton after Marion and set out alone on horseback for Snow's Island from her home just east of Camden, a forty mile journey, arriving the same day. She related her story to Marion after which he "secured a large comfortable tent for her and order for her a roast wild turkey dinner and a bottle of Horry's rare Italian wine. The following day a strong guard accompanied her home.

For the next incident, I will quote directly from Bobbie. "Mrs. Margaret Gordon, wife of Captain William Gordon of Marion's brigade learned of these plans while they were being discussed in Camden and as soon as she believed she had the essentials she made three copies of the plans as she had heard them and sent them by three of Marion's trustworthy scouts which had been stationed on the Gordon Plantation for just such a purpose. Mrs. Gordon gave each of them a fast horse and told them to "ride" which in the parlance of that time and place, meant to proceed as rapidly as possible. General Marion read the paper the scouts delivered and had his bugler sound assembly summoning every man on the island to his headquarters. He had been expecting some such move against him ever since Greene and Lee had left. His plans had all been made.

Marion sent out immediately his scouts along every road and trail from Snow's Island. They were sounding the summons "every man comes immediately with as much food as practical, but every man must come now." At the same time he sent a special messenger to his old friend John Nesmith, asking him to send him ten beeves (beef) dressed.

Francis Marion's training for warfare began as a young man; he would spend many days riding in the woods. He knew where all the good hiding places were and the location of the rivers and streams. He had a rice plantation in the Santee area of South Carolina.

Mouzon's map of 1775 shows the ferry at about the same location as the present Lynches River Bridge, just north of Johnsonville. In 1780, the ferry became the focus of Revolutionary War action. Marion organized an irregular force of raiders known as "Marion's Men." These men provided their own horses and food and came and went as the need to plant, cultivate, and harvest at home demanded. Marion lacked legal authority over the independent, half-equipped, and frequently hungry men, and they were often a thorn in his flesh. However, their skills as expert shooters, trackers, and hunters combined with Marion's tactical and leadership qualities provide a classic example of guerilla warfare. These two armies were to drive the Swamp Fox into his den and dig him out.

Witherspoon's Ferry

John Witherspoon was a founder and elder of Airwell Church. In the early 1800s, it lay in the path of expanding Methodism, which under the leadership of such ministers as Thomas Humphries and James Jenkins, was sweeping the lower Pee Dee. By 1815, this church had become all but extinct; and in 1818, the ferry lands reverted to the Witherspoon estates, coming under the ownership of David Rogerson Williams in the stead of his wife, Elizabeth, the daughter of John Witherspoon. Williams was a prominent South Carolinian. After serving a term as governor and two terms in the United States Senate, he turned his attention to internal improvements. He was responsible in 1820 for clearing the Pee Dee from Georgetown to Society Hill, this easing the burden that farmers bore in transporting their farm products to markets. Ten years later, he gathered workers and teams at the ferry for the purpose of constructing a bridge there. Such an improvement would have opened up large stretches of the backcountry. However, on November 17, 1830, Williams was killed at the ferry by falling timbers, and the bridge was not completed at that time. Williams' widow came into possession of the ferry lands, and upon her death in 1840, they passed to her stepson, John Nicholas Williams. In 1842, John Nicholas Williams sold the two tracts to William Johnson, who died in 1851, and his estate was settled in 1870. The executor's returns show rents for the ferry until 1870 when the real estate was divided among the heirs, and the ferry lands passed to his Woodberry grandchildren.

Johnsonville was part of Craven County (then a part of Williamsburg County), named after Lord Craven of England. On May 24, 1913, a charter was issued incorporating the town. During this time, Mr. Sylvester Briley Poston owned much of what is now city property. The rivers drew people as it was a way to travel. People would come from around to buy lots upon which to build houses, schools, churches, and businesses. Florence County was founded in 1888 from parts of Darlington, Marion, and Williamsburg counties. For many years, the Williamsburg County line was Lynches River. In 1921, Johnsonville went into Florence County. Excerpt from the book *As Time Goes By: Johnsonville and the Surrounding Areas* by Rebecca Hughes Dunahoe:

The ferry has a colorful past, with its associations with Francis Marion and Robert and John Dick Witherspoon, who were among Marion's most daring young officers. Local literature of the period continues to refer to the ferry. The first bridge to span the old ferry site was built about the turn of the century by Henry E. Eaddy.

After the fall of Charleston in the spring of 1780, the British quickly extended complete control of the South Carolina coast, including Georgetown, and began to place forces in posts upstate. A small force of regulars that had been to help in the defense of Charleston turned when they heard of Charleston's fall. Banastre Tarleton was sent to chase them. He caught up with them at Waxhaw and many of the troops were slaughtered although they had surrendered. South Carolina Governor Ruthledge had fled Charleston and the state "government" was wherever he happened to be hiding. At one time he went well into North Carolina to keep out of British hands. He sent several urgent appeals to Gen. George Washington for help.

Patrick Henry, 1775

They tell us, "Sir, we are weak, unable to cope with so formidable an adversary. But when shall we be stronger? Will it be the next week, or the next year? Will it be when we are totally disarmed, and when a British guard is stationed in every house? Shall we gather strength by irresolution and inaction? Shall we acquire the means of effectual resistance by lying supinely on our backs, and hugging the delusive phantom of hope, until our enemies shall have bound us hand and foot? Sir, we are not weak if we make proper use of those means which God of nature hath placed in our power.

"Three millions of people, armed in the holy cause of liberty, and in such a country as that which we possess, are invincible by any force which our enemy can send against us. Beside, Sir, we shall not fight our battles alone. There is a just God who presides over the destinies of Nations, and who will raise up friends to fight our battles for us. The battle, Sir, we have no election. If we were base enough to desire it, it is now too late to retire from the contest. There is no retreat but in submission and slavery! Our chains are forged! Their clanking may be heard on the plains of Boston! The war is inevitable; and let it come! I repeat, sir, let it come!

It is in vain, sir, to extenuate the matter. Gentleman may cry, "Peace, Peace!" but there is no peace. The war is actually begun! The next gale that sweeps from the north will bring to our ears the clash of resounding arms! Our brethren are already in the field! Why stand here idle? What is that gentlemen wish? What would they have? Is life so dear, or peace so sweet, as to be purchased at the price of chains and slavery? Forbid it, Almighty God! I know not what course others may take; but as for me, give me liberty or give me death!"

The Revolutionary War

One summer day on July 4, 1776, young Thomas Lynch came from Philadelphia to his plantation home on Lynch's River and told Williamsburg that he had, with some other South Carolinians, signed the Declaration of Independence on July 4, 1775 and that the thirteen colonies were at war with Great Britain. At this time he also visited the Hughes plantation, stated it was in pretty good shape for the area.

The revolution was in full swing. The Brittons and the Goddards were on the side of the Colonists. When Lieutenant Colonel Francis Marion came to Williamsburg to take command of the militia, the Snow's Island Goddards, Snows, Brittons, and Jenkins joined him. They had known the country along the Pee Dee Swamp had dense underbrush and knew of all the hiding places that were inaccessible to others, were invaluable to the Swamp Fox.

During the British stay in Philadelphia, Sir Henry Clinton began augmenting his forces by enlisting Americans in the provincial establishment, promising them the same pay, clothing, food, arms, and retirement as regulars from Britain. Lord Rawdon recruited a regiment from the Irishmen in the city and named it the Volunteers of Ireland. Sir Henry commissioned Rawdon the colonel and Wellbore Ellis Doyle as the lieutenant colonel of these Loyalist.

Lord Cathcart attempted to raise a regiment of Calendonian volunteers, and when that failed, Sir Henry turned the corps into the British Legion. He appointed Lord Cathcart the colonel and Major Banastre Tarleton the Lieutenant Colonel. Tarlston recruited four troops of light dragons and three companies of infantry. He then molded the British Legion into the most powerful striking force in the British Army.

When Sir Henry started his southern campaign in 1780, he continued to augment his forces with his provincial regiments. He assigned the command of the South Carolina Royalists to Colonel Alexander Innes, former secretary to Lord William Cambell, the last Royal Governor of South Carolina. He gave the American Volunteers to Lieutenant Colonel Patrik Ferguson and made him inspector of the Loyalists militia in South Carolina. Sir Henry captured Charleston on May 12, 1780, and then sent Lord Cornwallis and a powerful army to overrun the province. His lordship reached Camden on June 1. He wanted some local provincial regiments to help with populace.

In an attempt to win the people of Ninety-Six to the King's side, Cornwallis offered Robert Cunningham a major's commission on the Provincial forces if he would recruit a regiment of five hundred loyalists, but Ninety-Six's district was too rebellious. Cunningham failed. Nevertheless, he was later commissioned a brigadier general of Loyalist militia.

As soon as the arrival of Cornwallis at Camden became known, John Harrison, a planter who lived on Sparrow Swamp about three miles north of the present village of Lamar in Darlington County rode over to Camden and told his Lordship that he could recruit a regiment of five hundred men between Pee Dee and Santee.

Hoping to keep a loyalist's force between Camden and Georgetown, Cornwallis gave a commission to Harrison on June 4 and supplied him with blank commissions for the proposed officers. In honor of Lieutenant Colonel Thomas Brown's Florida Rangers, they named the unborn regiment the South Carolina Rangers. Major John Harrison immediately rode back to sparrow swamp and on June 6 swore in Robert Harrison and Samuel McConnell as lieutenant and two days later added Joel Hudson as Lieutenant. The Harrison's then chose the noncommissioned officers. They selected for Sergeant: Joseph Payne Jr., Joseph McKinney, John Eubanks and John Lewis. And for corporal: John Barr, Samuel Bennett, and James McFrail.

His staff completed, Major Harrison began swearing in the privates and by nightfall on June 8 had enlisted fifty-eight. Their names, preserved on the muster rolls of the South Carolina Rangers in the public archives of Canada in Ottawa are significant. Most of the surnames are English, thus revealing one of the sources of their loyalists. A few suggest the Scottish-Irish of Williamsburg, and there is an occasional Huguenot. Several appear to have brothers and one or two fathers and sons. Many of their names are still found along Lynches River.

In early August of 1780, General Horatio Gates, the American commander who had defeated the British at Saratoga, was marching a large army toward the British stronghold at Camden, South Carolina. Gates was supremely confident of inflicting another major defeat on the greatest military power in the world at the time. Francis Marion had been injured in Charleston a few months previously. Marion had been evacuated from Charleston due to his injury, thereby escaping capture by the British when they took Charleston. When Marion was sufficiently healed to travel, he gathered a small band of followers and set out for General Gates' camp near Camden, arriving some time after July 27, 1780. With his newly commissioned and noncommissioned officers and his fifty-eight recruits, Major Harrison marched up to Camden and went into camp. But he continued recruiting, and on June12, five more joined the South Carolina Rangers.

In the Governor's Palace in Williamsburg, Virginia, there is a map covering an entire wall illustrating Great Britain's colonies in North America in 1770. No doubt, in recognition for its famous indigo, the mapmaker printed the letters of Williamsburg Township so large and heavy that they dominate the northeast quarter of South Carolina. The coming revolution was to give the British a better reason to remember Williamsburg. It was the people of the King's Tree, Mingo, Nesmith, Snows Island near Lambert (in Hemingway] Witherspoon Landing (in Johnsonville), Lynches Creek, and the Indiantown area who formed the first partisan force to fight the British after the fall of Charles Towne in 1780. Under the leadership of Francis Marion, he wrote one of the great pages in American history.

"The women who stayed at home and managed their plantations while their men followed Marion; women who could ride and shoot as well as their husbands, and who proved their patriotism by daring deeds of heroism as well as by patient endurance. No less daring was Mrs. Jane Hawkins who was asked by seven British soldiers to direct them back to their camp, from which they had lost their way. Mrs. Hawkins mounted one of her horses, apparently to gratify them, and led them instead to be taken prisoners at Marion's headquarters, after having secured through pleasant conversation all the information she could.

"The daughters of those brave women were those whose unflagging courage during the days of the War has been immortalized in the inscription on the monument erected to their honor at the state capitol: Splendid in fortitude, they strove while they wept."

The proud record of the past is the inspiration of the future. Women of Williamsburg, you whose mothers nobly played their part in the making of this history, know that you are, today, co-makers of future history; and thank God for your heritage!

Colonel Ortho Williams of Gates Army gave this description of Marion and his men: "Colonel Marion, a gentleman of South Carolina, had been with the army a few days, attended by a very few followers, distinguished by small leather caps, and the wretchedness of their attire: their appearance was in fact so burlesque, that it was with much difficulty the diversion of the regular soldiery was restrained by the officers; and the General himself was glad of an opportunity of detaching Colonel Marion, at his own instance, toward the interior of South Carolina, with orders to watch the motions of the enemy and furnish intelligence."

Gates was apparently unimpressed, maybe even embarrassed by Marion's wretched little band and did not feel he needed Marion and his men to defeat the British at Camden. Gates therefore ordered Marion to leave the army at Camden, go south, burn boats, gather intelligence, and hamper a British retreat from command of the Williamsburg militia. On August 17, 1780, Marion and his little band left General Gates' army and began burning boats to cut off the expected British retreat from Camden. Marion's band reached the camp of the Williamsburg militia at Witherspoon's Ferry (present-day Johnsonville) on August 17, 1780. Marion assumed command of an eagerly awaiting Williamsburg Militia at Witherspoon's Ferry on August 17, 1780. Shortly after General Gates rid himself of Marion's little ragtag group, his army was virtually annihilated by the British at Camden. Gates had done Marion a great favor by sending him away and had set the stage for some of the greatest adventures and militia exploits in American history.

Francis Marion lay snug, a fox in his lair. After he had passed Britton's Ferry, the son of Widow Jenkins told him of a hiding place, high, dry, and inaccessible. He followed them through the Neck until they came to Dunham's Bluff, and from there they crossed over the Pee Dee to Snow's Island. They rode across the island to the plantation of William Goddard. William, a cousin of Francis Goddard, was about the same age as the Jenkins boys. He was an ardent Whig—patriotic, warmhearted, and willing to turn over his cabin, barn, and bins to the defenders of his country.

Marion found Snow's Island ideal for the headquarters of a partisan chief. Named for William Snow, an early settler of a Williamsburg, the island is a low ridge five miles long and two miles wide. Along its eastern shore runs the Pee Dee. Lynches River lies on the north, and along the western and southern borders runs Clark's Creek, one of the mouths of Lynches. To the west lie Snow's Lake and sloughs and morasses of Muddy Creek and Sockee Swamp.

William Goddard had built his house on the high ground toward the middle of the island, safe above the flood waters of the Pee Dee. On the ridges around his fields stood a virgin growth of gum and oak and pine, now gray and somber against the November sky. In the woods stood an undergrowth of bushes: dogwood, haw, and hornbeam, their branches entangled with brambles and wild muscadine vines. In the swamp and along the watercourses stood cypress trees like stately sentinels, their knees bare and their features hidden by streaming Spanish moss. On the side of the island was a long, impenetrable cane brake.

Marion pitched his camp in the woods near Goddard's cabin. The ridge was dry, the drainage good, and wood and water handy. With craft of frontiersmen, his men built crude lean twos for shelter. His mess sergeant he detailed Sergeant Davis whom he had rescued at Sumter's house. Aided by faithful Oscar, his black friend Davis became an enterprising caterer. To the almost constant diet of cornbread, beef, fresh pork, peas, and sweet potatoes, he added fish and game from the surrounding rivers and swamps.

As soon as the fury was over and the organization of the Brigade had settled, General Marion turned to routine duties. His failure to obtain powder, flint, or cartridge paper from Harrington or Greene or to capture any from the British supply boats had disarmed half of his men. Because of this constant shortage of ammunition, he had decided to convert part of his infantry into cavalry. Commandeering every whipsaw in Williamsburg, he set the blacksmith hammering out broad swords. Soon his horsemen were armed with long, keen, deadly weapons.

He then began recruiting. As his brigade increased, many of the Tories laid down their arms. Lukewarm patriots reaffirmed their allegiance: "Again to reconcile themselves to the cause they had first adopted and deserted with the utmost reluctance," William James noted, "And became confirmed in their views, by his apparent abilities and successes."

The general also began collecting provisions for his troops. Upon their return to Snow's Island the salt-collecting detachment had reported that the plantations in All Saints were still unrevised. The barns, cribs, and smokehouses were overflowing. Calling in Colonel Peter Horry, who knew every bypath on Waccamaw Neck, Marion concerted a plan to fill his larder. Writing out a set of orders similar to those given Captain Postell, he handed them to Horry. Then he reported to Greene: "I sent a detachment of forty men under Peter Horry to collect boats and drive off cattle."

Colonel Horry, Captain Clarke, Sergeant McDonald, and their troops crossed the Pee Dee near the house of Widow Jenkins, cut through the Back Swamp, and crossed the Little Pee Dee at Potato Bed Ferry. Before noon they crossed the Waccamaw below Kingston and cantered down into the Neck. As they were passing along Socastee Swamp, Sergeant McDonald spotted a splendid charger hidden in the swamp. Surrounding the horse with his squadron, he seized him.

Presenting him to Colonel Horry, he begged him to spare his own Janus.

As the detachment rode down Waccamaw Neck whooping, hallooing, and frightening the Tories, the advance patrol captured a man from the plantation of Captain William Allston. After questioning him, Horry placed him under guard. Soon afterward the party bivouacked near the Allston Plantation. During the night, Captain Clarke, who knew the slave, cut his bonds and sent him home. "Behold a militia captain releasing a prisoner confined by his colonel commandant," exclaimed Peter Horry wrathfully, "and see the consequences!"

Unknown to Horry, there was a troop of enemy horsemen on Waccamaw Neck. Angered by the recent salt raid, Colonel Campbell had sent sixty-five of the Queen's Rangers across Winyah Bay. As the Negro was slipping back to Allston's about sunrise, these Rangers picked him up. Frightened by their threats, the captive betrayed the presence of Horry's troops. Campbell immediately headed for their camp. But Peter Horry was vigilant. He was already moving forward and had sent Captain Clarke and five troopers ahead as advance guard. Spotting them, Campbell blew his horn.

"Stop!" cried Clarke to his men. "Wait and you will see the deer, dogs, and huntsmen as they cross the road!"

Before the hapless militia Captain recovered from his dream of chasing deer, some twenty of Merritt's veterans had put his party to flight and were hacking at his head. He surrendered. Colonel Campbell treated him with great courtesy and took his parole, only to see him take his heels and disappear behind the brambles and Jessamine vines of Waccamaw Swamp.

Alarmed by the noise of the scuffle, the rest of Colonel Horry's troops dashed up. They gave the Rangers a scattering blast of swan shot. At the sound, the captured horse bolted and threw Horry. Before he could run, a British sergeant bore down upon him with drawn sword. Fortunately, Horry's Continental uniform looked so much like that of a British lieutenant colonel that the ranger gave him a puzzled look, lowered his saber, and left him unscathed. The green-coated ranger then galloped away, and Horry supposed himself master of the field. Quickly he sent a detachment off with the prisoners. But to the colonel's surprise, Campbell dashed up with his entire command. Before Horry could catch his horse and mount, his men had scampered. Sergeant McDonald, seeing his commanding officer unhorsed, gave him his pony and then sprang into the somber morass of Socastee. "The promoted to Lieutenant Colonel by Congress, started creeping southward. He lingered in Richmond until December 15. Then, by easy marches averaging about ten miles a day, he passed along the wintry roads of North Carolina. "Colonel Lee is near at hand," Greene wrote Marion on January 4, in guarded reference to their secret plans. "I beg you to have collected all boats fit for transportation, down as low toward Georgetown as you may think if safe to send for them, and keep them in readiness until you hear further from me."

Light Horse Harry and his legion arrived at Camp Hicks on January 9, officers and men looking as if they had just come from a parade. "Col. Lee arrived yesterday, with his legion about 260," Rutledge wrote the South Carolina delegates. "I like him very much and expect great service from his corps."

Greene wrote Marion, "I wish your answer respecting the practicability of surprising the party near Nelson's." Then in routine fashion, he reported, "By the last accounts Lieut. Col. Tarleton was in motion, with about one thousand troops, toward Gen. Morgan, who is in the fork of Broad River."

At last able to spare the Continentals that Marion needed to stiffen the morale of his militia, Greene hustled off Colonel Lee down the Pee Dee. But the green uniform of his legionnaires, almost identical with those of Tarleton's Green Horse and Simcoe's Queen's Rangers, frightened the Whigs. They would tell him nothing about Marion's camp. So the colonel halted as Bass Mill on Catfish Creek and sent Major John Rudolph with a squadron to locate the elusive Swamp Fox.

As Lee's famed Continentals approached Snow's Island, Marion became perturbed. He realized that campaigning with young Harry Lee would raise delicate problems of command. The Carolina militia, with their loose discipline and their disdain of the regulars, would not take orders from the Virginian. And so, while Lee was still as Bass' Mill, the brigadier general settled the question of seniority. "Should I join in duty with him," he replied to a memorandum from Greene, "I expect to command, not from the Militia Commission I hold, but from an elder Continental Commission."

As Lee drew near, Marion sent an officer under a flag to Georgetown. His mission was ostensibly to return some letters captured from Major Irvine and to arrange prisoner exchange. But his instructions were to spy out conditions in Campbell's headquarters and to observe the state of the British garrison. Colonel Campbell received him civilly. "A Captain Clark of yours fell into my hands at the Waccamaw," he wrote Marion. "I have a right to except he will come and surrender himself as a prisoner of war; if he will come and surrender himself as a prisoner of war; if he has any spark of honor, he must, from my own generosity to him, think it a duty."

Lord Rawdon was alarmed by Colonel Lee's march from Camp Hicks with the finest combat team in the American Army. He feared that the maneuver foreshadowed an attack on Camden. With Tarleton beyond recall and Lord Cornwallis drawing away toward King's Mountain, he begged Leslie to remain with him for a few days. This delay in the march of the reinforcements had startling consequences. Instead of rushing on and cutting the Cherokee Road, thus forcing Morgan to retreat, Cornwallis waited for Leslie at Hillhouse Plantation on Turkey Creek. "I fear Morgan has too much the start of you," he wrote Tarleton on January 16. "Leslie will join me tomorrow or Thursday."

Unaware that Cornwallis had charged their plans, Tarleton was vigorously pushing his men westward. By swimming his horse and passing his men on foot logs, he crossed the swollen Enoree and Tyger Rivers. Crossing the Pacolet at Easterwood Shoals, before breakfast on January 15, he struck the American camp. Morgan immediately retreated to Burr's Mill on Little Thicketty Creek. On the night of January 16, he camped on an eminence known as the Cowpens.

At two o'clock on the morning of January 17, Tarleton began a rapid advance toward the Cowpens. Just before day an American patrol discovered his approach and dashed away to warn General

Morgan. The general began forming his lines of defense. Near the foot of the hill he established a cordon of skirmishers. About 150 yards above them, he posted Colonel Andrew Pickens and his Carolina militia. Among the oaks and the chestnuts across the ridge of Cowpens he stationed the Continentals commanded by Colonel Jonh Egar Howard; in a depression behind the ridge he hid Colonel William Washington and his dragoons.

Tarleton reached Cowpens about sunrise. Immediately he began marshaling his troops, the blended redcoats and green-coats forming a colorful line. On his far left stood Major Timothy Newmarsh's Seventh Regiment. The two hundred recruits that the Swamp Fox had frightened so badly, while Major McLeroth was shepherding them through Santee Swamp, were nervous and trembling. At Tarleton's command the British line began advancing while their two cannon sprayed the hillside with grapeshot. Uphill they charged, their officers shouting, "Give them the bayonet!" After Picken's militia fell back, Tarleton order Major McArthur's Highlanders to turn Howard's right flank. In wheeling to meet McArthur's attack, the Continentals fell into confusion. They then began retreating. Sensing victory, Tarleton threw everything into action, his infantry surging toward the Americans, his line straggling in tumultuous disorder.

(Bass, Robert D. Swamp Fox)

Morgan chose a new position and as the Continentals reached it, Howard shouted, "Face about! Give them one fire and the day is ours!"

The continentals came sharply about. They loosed a withering blast of buckshot from the hip. Howard shouted, "Give them the bayonet!"

Panic seized the British line. The recruits of the Seventh Regiment threw themselves on the ground and bellowed for quarter. Howard's troop charged through the hole they left in the line and began rounding up the British infantry. They captured both Newmarsh and McArthur, with their entire regiments. Banastre Tarleton saved only his Green Horse from the debacle.

"I have the particular pleasure to congratulate you on the entire defeat of the enemy under Lt. Col. Tarleton," Greene exultantly wrote Marion on January 23. "Major Giles, this moment's arrival brings the glorious intelligence."

Greene requested Marion to forward "this important intelligence" to Colonel Lee. "If he has not attacked Georgetown, I wish he could transmit it to the garrison." But even while the General was writing, Light Horse Harry and his Legion were moving toward Georgetown. On the evening of January 22, Captains Patrick Carnes and Michael Rudolph camped beside the militiamen on Snow's Island. At dawn they embarked ninety men in the flat-bottomed boats confiscated by Captain John Pastell and, guided by Marion's Rivermen, set off down the Pee Dee, with ninety miles of winding, icy river between them and Georgetown. All day and night they paddled and rowed and drifted. Before daylight on January 24, they reached the mouth of the Pee Dee River and concealed themselves on a small island at the head of Winyah Bay.

As soon as the water-borne contingent was under way, Marion began calling in his scouts, patrols, and detachments. "Particular circumstances make me desire that you will immediately march all the men under your command to join me at the Kingstree," he wrote Captain Postell. "You must proceed by forced marches until you come up to me, for no time is to be lost."

Having collected his men, on the evening of January 24, Francis Marion, with Henry Lee beside him, galloped down the road from Kingstree. But because of the bad roads they were late in reaching Georgetown. Before their arrival the infantry had begun operations.

When Lt. Col. Banastre Tarleton chased Francis Marion from Santee to Georgetown on November 8, 1780, the Snow's Island and Britton's Neck Goddards, Snows, Brittons, and Jenkins were with him. They quickly rode about ten miles from the ferry to Dunman's Bluff. Putting the men in boats and letting the horses swim along beside them, the Fox and his men crossed over to Snow's Island. Once there, they proceeded to William Goddard's plantation. In his book, Mr. James Jenkins says that Francis Marion used William Goddard's house as headquarters, and his men camped around the place. At William Goddard's plantation, Dr. Robert D. Bass said, "Francis Marion was in his den or lair!" The Swamp Fox was watchful and cautious and suspicious; he traveled by night, and he was at home in the swamps. The best known was Snow's Island. Yes, he was a fox! He would hit them and run to live and fight another day. He didn't fight clean, but he fought to win. He was brutal in that he looted, murdered, burned, and stole. At times, he was unappreciated. He was a shadowy figure using guerilla warfare. He and his Whigs stood alone against the British in lower South Carolina.

William Dobein James (1764–1830) was the youngest son of Major John James [1701-1750] and Elizabeth Witherspoon (1703–1750), the latter two being original Williamsburg settlers. To further confuse the issue, he was the brother of Captain John James. There are two others called John James in Williamsburg during this period. John, brother of William mentioned above [often designated John of Ox Swamp] and his son, "John of the Lake" complicated the names even further. Until the very last days, Marion never had more than several hundred men in the field at one time. They came when called if not too inconvenient and were quick to leave when the crops and the family needed them.

The South Carolina Rangers

In 1776, the British High Command decided to Americanize the war in the provinces of North America. They simply set Americans fighting over Americans. Their tactics in South Carolina succeeded in turning a revolution into a bloody war.

The Whigs were watching the mustering of these Tories and by the date had so badly wounded Angus McFrail that he had been placed in the general hospital in Camden. Harrison retaliated by scourging the Presbyterian community around Salem, Black River. His rangers killed several of the members, including elders of the church. Dr. Thomas Reese closed Salem Church, dismissed the students in his academy, and retired to Charlotte.

As Judge William Dobein James, who had been a student in the Salem Academy, wrote in his *A Sketch of the Life Brig. Gen. Francis Marion*: "Among these one shall be mentioned, the Rev. Dr. Thomas Reese of Salem on Black River. It was in his congregation that these murders perpetrated by Harrison and his followers first began, and three respectable men of his flock had already fallen victim of civil rage. Had he gone about to administer comfort out of his own family, it would have been termed sedition, and Dr. Reese would have made himself a voluntary martyr. He took the wiser course of retiring with his family before the storm..."

In his life, Judge James gives us our best information about the Harrisons, but his hatred of them makes him a biased witness. He wrote of the South Carolina Rangers, "These were headed by the two Harrisons, afterwards a colonel, the other major British service; whom Tarlatan calls men of fortune. They were in fact two of the greatest bandits that ever infested the country. Before the fall of Charleston they lived in a wretched log hut by the road, near

McCallam's in which there was no bed covering but the skins of wild beasts."

While this civil war raged along Black and Lynches Rivers, Harrison and his staff continued to recruit. On June 24, 1780, John Jenkins, deputy muster and master for the provincial forces, came to the camp of the rangers for a muster and inspection. He reported that there were in South Carolina Rangers one major, two captains, two lieutenants, one ensign, four sergeants, three corporals, and eighty privates. Jenkins dated his report "near Camden," but the rangers must have been somewhere near Radcliff's Bridge some six or seven miles down Lynches River from present Bishopville.

The report of Muster Master Jenkins so pleased Lord Cornwallis that on June 30, 1780, he wrote Sir Henry Clinton, "I have agreed to a proposal make by Mr. Harrison, to raise a provincial corps of five hundred men, with the rank of Major, to be composed of thee natives of the country between to Pee Dee and Wateree, and which it is extremely probable that he will succeed."

But there was a movement afoot on which Cornwallis did not count. Baron DeKalb with seven thousand was marching toward Camden. As he had passed through North Carolina, two ragged Continental officers named Francis Marion and Peter Horry had joined his troops. When they were twelve miles above Camden, General Horatio Gates detached the two Huguenots and sent them to supervise the militia in Williamsburg. On the next day, Gates threw his army against that of Lieutenant General Earl Cornwallis and was decisively defeated. The British troops captured a thousand prisoners.

As Cornwallis wrote Sir Henry, he fought the battle of Camden only to save eight hundred British soldiers ill with fever. Afraid that the epidemic of Malaria would spread to the prisoners, he began sending them to Charlestown in batches of one hundred and fifty. Francis Marion with several companies of Williamsburg Militia was on a boat burning foray up the Santee. On the night of August 24, 1780, the day that Muster Master Jenkins was paying his second visit to the South Carolina Rangers, Marion surprised the guards of the first batch of prisoners at the house of Colonel Thomas Santee near

Nelson's Ferry. He released the prisoners and flew towards Kingstree. Late on the afternoon of August 25, he crossed Lynches River at Witherspoon's Ferry and headed toward Ports Ferry on Pee Dee River.

Militia played many roles during the campaign fought in the Carolinas in the War of American Independence. They attacked British detachments and outpost, overawed loyalists, and captured supply ships on the Santee and Congaree Rivers. Among their less glamorous duties, they collect cattle, salt, and provisions for their own use and to prevent them from falling into the hands of the British. They also collected intelligence for Generals Horatio Gates and Nathanael Green. Finally, though they were better prepared for guerrilla warfare than for participation in pitched battles, they sometimes fought on major actions, but with mixed results. They fought like battle-tested veterans at Cowpen and Eutaw Springs, but they were routed at the battle of Camden.

Although the part-time soldiers fought well at Cowpens and Eutaw Springs, it is fair to say that their most valuable services were performed on a day-to-day basis in their own neighborhoods. There they kept loyalists from joining the British, collected provisions for use of the American army, and harassed the British in every possible way. In doing so they acted, in the words of Professor John Shy of the University of Michigan, as "the sand in the gears of the [(British)] pacification machine."

To be sure, the British were sometimes able to drive Marion and his followers into hiding in the swamps. But the "Swamp Fox" was able to return to the field after the sweeps that were designed to destroy his brigade.

Professor Rankin had done justice to Marion's leadership qualities including his ability to rebound from adversity, and he has been particularly careful to separate fact from fiction about the general's exploits. Happily, Marion's combat record emerges as a very creditable one even after fiction and hero-worshiping have been cast aside. His victories were far more numerous than his reverses, and they enabled him to control a large area between the Pee Dee and Santee Rivers even when the American army in the South had been driven so far into North Carolina that it could give him no direct support.

The emergence of Francis Marion upon the Santee, from a firm base among the Whigs of Williamsburg, and with followers drawn from the country along Pee Dee River, stirred Lord Cornwallis to punitive steps. He ordered Major James Wemyss to march his battalion of the Sixty-Third Regiment from the High Hills of Santee to Kingstree. On August 28, he wrote, "I should advise you sweeping the country entirely from Kingstree Bridge to Pee Dee, returning by the Cheraw's."

Major Wemyss and his troops knew little of the topography of South Carolina, and so Cornwallis ordered Major Harrison and his Rangers to join Wemyss. They knew the roads, rivers, creeks, ferries, and fords; therefore, they were invaluable as guides, scouts, and couriers. They also knew the other loyalists and could lead the British to the homes of Rebels.

Wemyss and Harrison marched into Williamsburg. At Kingstree, they went on a rampage. Wemyss burned the Presbyterian Church at Indiantown, snorting, "This is a sedition shop." He then led his troops to the home of Major John James. The major and son William Dobein were in Marion's camp in white Marsh North Carolina. Hoping to lure Major James to try and rescue his family, Wemyss locked Mrs. James and her children in their home for two days. He then released them and burned the house before their eyes. William Dobein never forgave Wemyss; he carried an undying hatred for the Harrisons.

With Harrison's rangers leading the way, Major Wemyss then burned a swath fifteen miles wide between Kingstree and Cheraw. In this report, dated September 20, 1780, Wemyss wrote, "I have done everything in my power to get at Mr. Marion" and then he summarized the situation in Williamsburg: every family involved, the women sullen, the men run off with Marion, and the slaves hiding out. Then in a postscript he added, "I forgot to tell your lordship that I have burnt and lay to waste about fifty houses and plantations.

On September 24, 1780, Lord Cornwallis marched the British Army into Charlotte in what he expected would be in the beginning of the subjugation of North Carolina. There he remained more than a month in reorganizing the loyalists' militia and deploying the provincial regiments and strategic positions in South Carolina. He ordered Major Wemyss to move to Camden with the Sixty-Third regiment and to leave Harrison and his South Carolina Rangers posted at Cheraw. To reinforce Harrison's regiment he sent Major Thomas Fraser with eighty mounted men to the South Carolina Royalist regiment in "hope he will be able with the help of the militia of the lower districts to secure the country tolerable well."

In obedience to the order of Lord Cornwallis, Wemyss began preparing to return to Camden, and he decided to take the South Carolina Rangers back to their camping ground. On September 30, 1780, he wrote Cornwallis of his decision excusing his " presuming in regard to Harrison's Corps to disobey your directions, being convicted that were they left here, that they would dispense in two or three days. They are if possible, worse than militia, their sole desire being to plunder and steal, and when they have got as much as their horses will carry, to run home."

Back in their camp near Radcliff's, the South Carolina Rangers found that Francis Marion had returned from White Marsh and, on September 2, 1780, had destroyed the loyalists' militia of Colonel John Coming Ball at Black Mingo. He was campaigning freely between the Pee Dee and Santee.

Colonel Balfour ordered Colonel Benjamin Tynes to muster the militia along Black River. Colonel Marion learned of the assembly at Tear Coat Swamp between Black and Pocatalico Rivers. He rode into Kingstree and spread a rumor that he was going up Lynches River to chase Harrison and his Rangers. On the night of October 26, he fell upon the regiment of Tynes, sending them squandering so fast that eighty of them left their horses, saddles, and muskets.

Judge James wrote, "His first intention was to chastise Harrison on Lynches Creek and he was moving up for that purpose." This is the only reference to the location of Harrison's camp. The British next assigned Harrison and his South Carolina Rangers the duty of patrolling the country between Santee and Pee Dee Rivers and keeping a check over the guerrillas under Francis Marion. When Lieutenant Colonel Banister Tarleton set out from Camden with his green horse on November 4, 1780, to drive Marion from the supply line along the Santee; he called on the South Carolina Rangers to serve as guides, couriers, and provisionary.

Harrison's rangers were with Tarleton on the morning on November 8, 1780, when the Green Dragon chased Francis Marion from Jack's Creek to Ox Swamp, in present Clarendon County, and cursed him for a "damned old fox." They spread the story and helped to popularize the nickname Swamp Fox.

The Rangers guided Tarleton and the dragoons off the British Legion for twenty-five miles through swamps, woods, and fastnesses toward Black River without halt," Tarleton reported to Lord Cornwallis. In his Campaign Report, dated or Singleton's Mills (Poinsettia State Park), he devoted only one sentence to the rangers: "A few prisoners were taken from the Swamps by Col. Harrison's Corps."

Upon his return from chasing the Swamp Fox, however, the Green Dragoon was lavish in his praise of the South Carolina Rangers. Lord Rawdon, who on November 13, has assumed command in Camden, reported to Lord Cornwallis, "I hear much of the prowess of Harrison's Rangers, upon the Expedition with Tarleton: A valiant friend of government is a prodigy of which the world talks."

But in his secret cipher, the young Irish Lord confirmed the opinion of James and Wemyss that the South Carolina Rangers were a banditti who lacked discipline: "They want to plunder and not do regular duty."

During their campaigning the South Carolina Rangers began suffering casualties. On October 14, 1760, Captain Robert Harrison was killed. Whether the captain was brother or father of Major Harrison is not known. But his death led to a vendetta that became barbaric. In December, Private Benjamin Payne was killed. On December 2, both William and Stephen Parish fell to Marion's men. On December 5, Lord Rawdon wrote Cornwallis, "Two brothers of Major Harrison, who were ill of the Small Pox, lay at a house about eight miles in our rear. Last night a scouting party of Rebels burst into the house; shot both of the sick men in their beds, though they were incapable of making the least defense."

Toward the end of December, Lieutenant Colonel John Watson Tadwell-Watson, an officer in the Third Regiment of Guards, brought the Provincial Light Infantry, a loyalist regiment recruited around New York, down to Charlestown. Before his arrival, Lord Cornwallis assigned Watson to the command of Lord Rawdon who decided to put him chasing Marion. To lead the fresh troops to the lair of the Swamp Fox, Rawdon called in the South Carolina Rangers. Harrison met Watson at Nelson's Ferry and guided him up the Santee to an old Indian mound. Watson was pleased with the site and started building a little bastion which he named Fort Watson. To help defend the fort, Major Harrison detached Ensign Richard Lewis and a squad of twelve privates.

On February 8, 1780, soon after Watson had garrisoned the little ford, General Thomas Sumter, on a foray down the Santee, tried to storm the bastion. Repulsed and driven off, Sumter led his troops to his old home in the High Hills, secured his wife and son, and set off toward the Waxhaw's. At Stirrup Branch, he met a party of Fraser's South Carolina Royalists. "Yesterday Fraser met Slater, who was advancing this way, between Scrape Hoar and Radcliffe's Bridge" Rawdon informed Watson on March 7, 1781. "A smart action ensued, in which the enemy were completely routed, leaving ten dead upon the field and forty wounded." Sumter fled across Radcliff's Bridge and then burned the structure. It was never rebuilt.

Having driven Sumter from the Santee, Rawdon determined to chase Marion out of Snow's Island. He initiated a two-pronged drive - Watson to fight and pin down Marion's troops and Doyle and the Volunteers of Ireland to cut in behind the fighting and destroy Marion's camp on Snow's Island.

Early on the morning of March 5, 1781, Colonel Watson with his Provincial Light Infantry, the Sixty-Fourth Regiment, and the South Carolina Rangers marched from Fort Watson. At Wiboo Swamp about halfway between Nelson's and Murray's ferries he met the guerilJas under Marion. In bloody, hand-to-hand fighting, they drove Marion from the Wiboo Swamp.

Marion retreated to Kingstree, crossed Black River, threw the planks off the bridge, and defied Watson to cross. After two weeks,

Watson made a dash toward Georgetown. Marion caught him at the bridge over Sampit River. Here in vicious fighting the South Carolina Rangers behaved like the veterans they were. But it was their last battle. Watson did not reach Camden in time to fight at Hobkirk's Hill.

Across the South Carolina backcountry, hundreds of women took sides in the revolution, feeding and supplying the militia, tending the sick and wounded, and providing intelligence. As bitter partisan warfare raged, stories of women who stood up to the British and loyalist forces spread rapidly and were a source of encouragement for the hard-pressed Whigs. Rebecca Motte, a prominent window of Charleston and St. Matthew Parish, provided one such dramatic story.

Rebecca Brewton Motte came from a family of wealthy slave traders and revolutionaries in Charleston. Her brother, Miles Brewton, was a leader in the revolutionary movement until his death at sea in 1775. She and her husband, Jacob Motte, furnished the Whig militia with food and fodder. When the British captured Charleston in May 1780, they chose her family home on Kings Street, widely regarded as one of the finest in the province, as their headquarters. After her husband's death, she and her daughter retreated to their summer home in St. Matthews Parish. Mount Joseph plantation was below McCord's Ferry on the Wateree, near its confluence with the Congaree toform the Santee.

But as partisan warfare engulfed the backcountry, Rebecca Motte again found herself at the center of the conflict. Because of its strategic location, early in 1781, the British took over Mount Joseph and converted it into a fortress. To the natural strength of Motte's house, British engineers added a moat, earthworks, and strong palisades of sharpened tree trunks. Inside were stationed Lt. Donald McPherson with some 150 men, mostly British and Hessians, and a generous store of gunpowder. Because it could be reduced by siege or cannon fire, the fort became the principal depot for the convoys moving supplies from Charleston to Camden. Motte and her children were consigned to another on the plantation, probably the overseer's house.

After their successful attack on Fort Watson, Francis Marion and Lighthorse Harry Lee decided to move against Fort Motte. On May 8, 1781, they surrounded the fort. They had just begun to dig siege tranches when they received word that Lord Rawdon had abandoned Camden and was en route to Fort Motte. On the night of May 11, McPherson's beleaguered troops gave a shout of triumph. They could see Rawdon's campfires twinkling in the High Hills.

"If it were a place," she replied, "it should go." Several sources indicate that Motte then presented them with a special East Indian bow and flaming arrows, a gift to her from her brother, to do the job.

After waiting until noon when the roof had become hot and dry, Lee ordered a marksman to begin shooting flaming arrows. Soon the housetop was ablaze in several places. As the flames began to crackle, McPherson sent a detail up to rip off the burning shingles. The Whigs' single cannon fired away at them, and with men jumping from the roof into the moat, McPherson hurriedly raised a white flag. As soon as the British cast down their arms, Marion sent some of his men to douse the flames. He treated the imperial troopsand the loyalist militiamen with kindness.

Immediately after the surrender, Rebecca Motte invited both the American and the British officers to dine with her. In order to accommodate so many guests, she and her slaves set the table under an arbor in front of her cabin.

As Peter Horry recalled, "For my life I could not keep my eyes from her. To think what an irreparable injury these officers had done her! And yet, to see her, regardless of her own appetite, selecting the choicest pieces of the dish, and helping them with the endearing air of a sister, appeared to me one of the loveliest spectacles I had ever seen. It produced the happiest effect on us all. Catching her amiable spirit, we seemed to have entirely forgotten our past animosities, and Britons and Americans mingled together, in smiles and cheerful chat, like brothers."

During the dinner, General Marion was alerted that some of Lee's men were executing Tories. He sprang up from the table, grabbed his sword, and ran downhill towards his camp. He met with a grisly scene: two men were lying dead on the ground, and another

Tory named Levi Smith was hanging by the neck from the beam of the garden gate.

"Cut him down! Cut him down!" yelled Marion. "In the name of God, what are you doing?"

"Only hanging a few Tories, sir," replied Cornet William Harrison of Colonel Lee's dragoons.

"I'll let you know, damn you," Marion shouted, "that I command here and not Colonel Lee!"

On April 14, 1781, Francis Marion with his militia and Light House Harry Lee with his legion rendezvoused at the Santee River to try to capture the fort. Neither the defenders of the fort nor the patriots besieging it had cannon. Lacking entrenching tools needed to dig and construct siege works, the patriots were making very slow progress against the fort. Having no water inside the walls, the British defenders dug a well. The patriots could not successfully storm the fort without suffering heavy losses and the British defenders could not escape. The patriots, originally hopeful of a quick victory, were faced with a standoff. Worse, the longer the siege continued, the greater the chance the British would send a force to rescue the fort.

A solution to the stalemate was proposed to Marion by Lieutenant Colonel Hezekiah Maham. On April 20, Maham suggested the patriots construct a tower taller than the fort so that marksmen could shoot into the fort from above. The plan was immediately accepted. The patriots began scouring nearby plantations for axes and then began cutting pine saplings. An oblong tower was constructed out of range of the British muskets. A floor was built inside the tower at a point higher than the top of the fort's wall and the tower was reinforced and shielded with timber. The structure was completed on April 23. Expert marksmen from McCottrey's rifles climbed to the top and at dawn began firing down into the Fort. Buckshot from the British muskets could not penetrate the tower but bullets from the rifles sprayed into the fort. Under cover of the rifles in the tower, the Patriots removed a section of abatis and began tearing at the logs forming the fort's walls. Light Horse Harry Lee's Legion, bayonets fixed and helmets down, stood ready to force their way into the fort once the logs were removed. At this time the fort's defenders raised a white flag and subsequently surrendered.

Maham's tower resulted in the destruction of a critical link in the British communications and supply chain. Francis Marion and Light Horse Harry Lee lost only two killed and suffered six wounded. This was the first time a British fort had been taken since the invasion of South Carolina. The invention of Hezekiah Maham would be used again in the Revolutionary War, but never with better results.

"I have appointed Col. Marion a Brigadier and thrown all the regiments eastward of Santee, Wateree, and Catawba into his Brigade," Governor Ruthledge wrote the South Carolina delegates in Congress on December 30, 1780. A courier with a letter from the governor, posting rapidly down the Pee Dee from Thomas's Plantation nearly opposite Cheraw Hill, reached Snow's Island on New York's Day, (January 1781). Marion opened the letter from the governor. His dark eyes lighted up, and a smile spread over his swarthy face. He handed the paper to Peter Horry. "As soon as I came to his new title 'Brigadier General,' said Horry, "I snatched his hand and exclaimed, 'Huzza! God save my friend my noble General Marion.

Governor Ruthledge had appointed Francis Marion Brigadier General because of his rare abilities. As a Continental officer he had rallied, inspired, and led the militia to victory after victory. He was a sound strategist, a keen tactician, and a savage fighter. He had surpassed every other leader in spreading terror among the Tories between the Santee and the Little Pee Dee.

He was a stern disciplinarian, observing and demanding the highest standards of militia efficiency. And yet he was kind, humane, and thoroughly sympathetic to his suffering, ill-equipped followers. Since they had no tents, he also slept in the open. He was bold to the verge of audacity, and yet he took no unnecessary chances, protecting his men and himself from all avoidabletrouble. They followed him with admiration and devotion.

Excitement soon spread through the woodland camp at Goddard's. Brigadier General Marion had begun organizing his Brigade. From his band of heroes he appointed Captain John Milton his aide, and for junior aides chose Captain Lewis Ogier and Captain

Thomas Elliott. Captain Elliott took charge of the General Greene, Governor Ruthledge, and the Whigs leaders became firm and regular.

General Marion appointed Colonel Hugh Ervin, the senior officer of the militia, second in command of his cavalry, and Horry formed his regiment of the troops commanded by Major Lemuel Benson and Captains John Baxter, John Postell, Daniel Conyers, and James McCauley. Marion also gave the regiment nominally commanded by Colonel Adam McDonald, then a prisoner on parole, to lieutenant Colonel Hough Horry. Hugh Horry's subordinates included Major John James, Captain John James, Captain James Postell, and Captain James Witherspoon.

Then, with Colonel Hugh Horry and Captain James Postell, trusted Huguenot counselors, Marion formed a mess. For huts, lean-to style, to protect them against wind and rain. For their scant stores of food and militia supplies they built storage bins. For their prisoners they strengthened Goddard's barn and, with soldiers' humor, named it the bull pen. To prevent surprise, the Swamp Fox drew all boats to his side of the rivers and destroyed those he did not need. To further insulate his retreat, he had his men fell trees into the fords, remove puncheon from the causeways, and break down the bridges over the creeks and branches in Williamsburg.

Marion also ordered Colonel John Ervin to throw up a small redoubt on the lower side of Dunham's Bluff, and garrison it with a guard from Captain John Dozier's company of Britton's Neck militia. Safe, well provisioned, and located in a strategic position, he then called in those militiaman who could be trusted with a knowledge of his rendezvous. As his regiment swelled, he began sending out foragers and scouts. Soon his camp was like a beehive. Far and wide his patrols ranged, their way lighted only by the stars and the moon, and soon the hoofs of their horses had worn new trails into Snow's Island.

McLeroth left Kingstree and marched near Nelson's Ferry, but yesterday I hear he was on his return to Kingstree again, he was reinforced with 150 militia from south of Santee," Marion wrote Gates from his new headquarters on "Linches Creek near PeeDee." "Tynes who I had taken, with several others in the British services & sent to Gen'l. Harrington made their escape from him and is again

Embodying the militia to the high hills of Santee, with an Intention to reinforce Maj. McLeroth, this will give the Maj'r a superiority in this part of the country and I shall be obliged to retreat."

Marion was inexorable in his orders that his scouting parties refrain from violence. He would not countenance useless bloodshed. But loyalists could be subjected to terrors, and marauding bands of Whigs committed every kind of barbarity. "Two brothers of Major Harrison's, who were ill of the smallpox, lay at a house about eight miles in our rear," Rawdon informed Cornwallis on December 5, 1781. "Last night a scouting party of Rebels burst into the house, shot both of the sick men in their beds, Though they were incapable of making the least defense."

Alert, restless, never remaining at any spot long enough for the Tories to guide the British to his camp, Marion left Benbow's Ferry and marched back to the Santee. The weather was mild, and the countryside a wintry gray, soft and pleasant. He was genial, and his troops were in good spirits. Everyone had a consciousness of sacrificing self-interest for a noble cause.

In addition to the Swamp Fox's fine record of raising men, training them, and leading them in combat, it should be noted that he served as an intelligence officer for General Greene during the final month of 1780 and a large part of 1781 and 1782. A study of his letters to Greene shows that, trained for it or not, Greene, who commanded the American army after the departure of General Gates, ordered Marion to forward intelligence to him about British troop movement, troop strength, losses in combat and from disease, and all other matter which might have a bearing on forthcoming militia operations.

Greene's request for intelligence must have been a burden to an officer who had troubles enough in raising, training, and leading a brigade of farmers, planters, and blacksmiths. Marion had no training in gathering and evaluating intelligence. Indeed, he had no training in the rules of evidence and was for a time careless about distinguishing between facts and hearsay. Yet he was willing to give Greene such help as he could. "I shall," he wrote to his superior, "endeavor to procure intelligence as you desire, but shall meet with great difficulty, as nothing but gold or silver passes here, and I am destitute of either." Despite the lack of hard money with which to pay spies and couriers, he promised, "When anything occurs worthwhile I shall acquaint you with it by way of the post at the Cheraws on Pee Dee."

True to his word, Marion sent several letters to Greene each week with intelligence about British strength and movement. For example, he reported on one occasion that "a party of the Enemy under Major McLeroth with two hundred infantry and two field pieces went up to the high hills of Santee, with which I skirmished and killed and wounded six, one Captain Kelley of the Sixty-Fourth. Regiment." In dozens of letters, which followed, he reported similar information. Following rules of evidence which he learned from experience, he supplied regimental designations where possible, troop strength, number of artillery pieces accompanying the enemy, and enemy's losses when he was able to ascertain them.

To Marion's credit, he rarely sent Greene rumors of victories or defeats in faraway places. He usually confined himself to reporting facts which he or some of his officers had observed. For example, he reported almost daily upon the movements made by several battalions of infantry, commanded by Major-General Alexander Leslie, which marched from Charleston to Winnsboro in January 1781 to reinforce the British field army.

It was of the highest importance for Greene to know of the approach of Leslie's redcoats. For Greene's army was numerically weak and was poorly equipped in January, on the eve of the battle of Cowpens. Moreover, a part of the army had been detached, under command of Brigadier General Daniel Morgan, to threaten the loyalists in the Ninety-Six District. Morgan's detachment faced mortal danger if Charles, Lord Cornwallis, who commanded the British army at Winnsboro, should launch a reinforced by Leslie's detachment.

Fortunately for Greene and Morgan, Marion was able to send accurate information about the progress of the redcoats as they toiled through rain and mud toward Winnsboro. To be sure, officers other than Marion—Thomas Sumter among them—forwarded intelligence of Leslie's march to Greene. But Marion was the first militia leader to learn of the arrival of Leslie's troops in South Carolina. Likewise, he was the first officer to learn of the departure of the redcoats from Charleston when they commenced their mud-spattered march inland.

Thanks to the timely intelligence which he had received from Marion and Sumter, Greene was able to escape from Cornwallis' grasp when the earl invaded North Carolina after Leslie's troops had joined him. Greene's army and Morgan's detachment, elated by its victory at Cowpen but Dan River in the nightmarish march through rain and sleet. But Greene was reinforced heavily after he had retired into Virginia. And Cornwallis's troops, having marched far from their bases, received no replacements for the losses which they had suffered from the rigors of the winter campaign.

With his army strengthened, Greene became the hunter instead of the hunted. He again crossed the Dan and followed his adversary to the wooded slopes at Guilford Court House. At that place he drew up his troops in preparation for battle and waited hopefully for Cornwallis to attack him. The earl obliged. Frustrated by the apparent failure of his offensive, he accepted Greene's challenge. In the desperate and bloody battle which followed, his lordship's troops succeeded n driving the American army from the field. Yet their victory was a pyrrhic one. They lost 532 officers and men killed and wounded from the 1,924 who had been committed to battle. Of the hundred officers who had seen action, twenty-nine were killed or wounded and two regimental commanders died of their wounds.

Among Greene's Continentals regulars the losses were less severe than among Cornwallis's redcoats. To be sure, some eight hundred of Greene's militia were missing after the battle. Since they had not been taken prisoner, it appears that they had gone home to their wives and sweethearts. Even with their departure, however, the American army was numerically superior to Cornwallis' shattered force. Thus, the victorious British were obliged to retreat southward shortly after the battle. Not surprisingly in the circumstances, Greene promptly occupied the battlefield and then resumed his pursuit of the British.

Guilford Court House proved to be a major turning point in the war in the Carolinas. It crippled Cornwallis' army, and it led to the reoccupation of the South Carolina by Greene's troops.

If Cornwallis had led the remnants of his army into South Carolina, Greene might have encountered serious opposition to his army from the Carolinas by leading it into Virginia. After the battle at Guilford Court House, he had retreated to Cross Creek (now Fayetteville). Finding little support there from the loyalists, he had his weary redcoats down the valley of the Cape Fear River to Wilmington. Finally, after giving his sick and wounded a much-needed rest, he had decided to march to Virginia, there to unite his army with a strong detachment commanded by Major General William Phillips.

Meanwhile, Greene struck out on a course of his own. After following his opponent for several days, he veered from Cornwallis' trail and began to march toward Camden. In doing so, he commenced the process of toppling the structure of British outposts and supply lines in South Carolina. He led American's Southern army into the parts of the state in which the irregulars commanded by Francis Marion and Thomas Sumter exercised considerable control. Thus, Marion's men and Sumter's found themselves fighting in the front lines after several months of strenuous partisan warfare in Cornwallis's zone of the interior.

As the American army advanced into South Carolina, its commanding general took steps to cooperate with Marion and Sumter. He sent a detachment of dragoons and mounted infantry, commanded by Lieutenant-Colonel Henry Lee, to aid Marion. Outpostswere taken one by one as Marion and Lee carried out a series of successful siege operations. A small British post, called Fort Watson, was the first to fall. Before the end of April, Marion was able to send Greene the entire garrison with all their arms and ammunition.

While Lee and Marion were occupied with siege operations, Greene was unable to march to their aid because he was held in check by the garrison of Camden, commanded by Francis. Because of the havoc which Lee and Marion inflicted upon his supply lines, Rawdon was obliged to evacuate Camden. Before he did so, however, Greene was dependent upon Marion for intelligence about British defense in the interior of South Carolina. Moreover, when Rawdon's veteran infantry retreated, Marion furnished Greene with accurate information about its movements to the south side of the Santee River.

After occupying Camden, Greene advanced to support Lee and Marion. But he did not remain with them for long; instead, he led his army westward to besiege the fort at Ninety Six. He hoped to capture it before Lord Rawdon could march to its relief, but the garrison resisted stubbornly and the siege dragged on through several weeks of May and June. Meanwhile, several battalions of British infantry arrived at Charleston from the British Isle. Rawdon, who was young and energetic, selected the best troops from among the new arrivals and led them on a series of forced marches through hot, muggy weather to save the beleaguered garrison.

As the British army marched out of Charleston on its rescue mission, it fell to Marion's lot to send the unwelcome but important news to Greene. As the redcoats hurried westward, first Marion and then Sumter forwarded information of their advance. Thus, Greene was aware that a relief column was on its way to interfere with his siege operations. Unfortunately, he reacted to Rawdon's approach somewhat unwisely. In a desperate effort to capture the fort before it could be relieved, he ordered his troops to carry it by storm. But the garrison fought valiantly, and the attacks were beaten off with heavy losses.

Despite the defeat which they had suffered, Greene's Continentals were able to occupy Ninety Six soon after Rawdon's army had rescued its garrison. His lordship was obliged to order the defenders of the fort to evacuate the ramparts which they had defended so gallantly. Marion's capture of Fort Watson and a number of other British posts in the valleys of the Congaree and Wateree had severed the supply lines between Ninety Six and the British bases in the low country. So the brave defenders of Ninety Six retired from their frontier post, and Greene followed them and their rescuers eastward into the low country.

When the opposing armies had reached the lowlands, Marion was able to make himself particularly useful to his superior. For the war had moved into Marion's backyard. With his customary zeal for the cause of independence, the Swamp Fox continually with the Britishwhen he could find time to do so, raising men, training them, and collecting cattle and provisions for the American army.

Perhaps the most important of Marion's services during the summer of 1781 was the collecting of food and fodder for the use of Greene's troops, and for the purpose of preventing the British from getting them. Driving cattle and carrying off supplies of corn, rice, and salt was hardly glamorous work; but it had to be done. Marion's men rode widely through the country south of the Santee on their foraging missions. As Marion explained in a letter to Greene, his patrols had orders to gather provisions and keep the British "so close" to Charleston "that they will not be able to get any Subsistence from the Country." Moreover, as he mentioned in his letter, he had ordered his foragers to drive all the cattle they could find to the north side of the Santee. Thus, if the British should drive his patrols from the field, they would find the larder empty.

Busy as he was with skirmishing, foraging, and raising men, Marion continued to collect intelligence. He had become increasingly careful to verify information which he sent to his superior. For example, he had learned that prisoners and deserters were likely to supply misinformation. Therefore, it was necessary to send scouts or patrols to check on intelligence gained from such unreliable informants. For example, when Lord Rawdon's army encamped at Orangeburg after its return from Ninety Six Marion sent a patrol, commanded by Major Maham, to keep watch upon it. Maham learned everything he could about the British from local inhabitants, British stragglers, and close observation of the enemy's camp. From these sources, including two stragglers whom his men captured, he learned that the British "are so fatigued they cannot possible move." And Marion forwarded Maham's report of the exhausted state of Rawdon's army to Greene, knowing that it was based on information from several sources and knowing also that the British had just returned from marching more than three hundred miles through hot, humid summer weather.

Maham's information about the exhausted state of the British army was important because it indicated that Rawdon was unable to take the offensive. Many of Rawdon's soldiers were sick as a result of the hardships of their march to Ninety Six, and Rawdon himself became so ill that he was obliged to relinquish his command to sail for England to recuperate.

Because of the severity of the summer campaign, the American army was as nearly exhausted as was Rawdon's. Yet its commander was so determined to drive the British into Charleston that he thought seriously of attacking Orangeburg. He changed his mind quickly, however, for two reasons. For one thing, he learned upon reconnoitering the town that there were several brick buildings in it which the redcoats could use as impromptu forts. For another, thanks to intelligence-gathering by Maham and Marion, he had been furnished with a list of the battalions in Orangeburg with a statement of their strength. By comparing the strength of his army with the list of Rawdon's troops, Greene was able to learn at a glance that he enjoyed only a slight numerical advantage over his adversaries.

After giving up all hope of attacking Orangeburg. Greene withdrew his regulars to the High Hill of Santee where they could rest during the remainder of the sickly season. He allowed no rest for his militia, however; evidently convinced that Marion's followers and Sumter's could march and fight in summer weather, he ordered them to dislodge the British from their posts at Dorchester and Monks Corner.

In compliance with his superior's orders, Marion became involved in some heavy fighting in July and August. In one action, at Quinby Bridge, he lost nine officers and men killed and eighteen wounded in a determined attack upon troops who were sheltered in houses and behind rail fences. Despite his participation in combat, however, he continued to send patrols and scouts to gather intelligence for his own use and that of General Greene. At the beginning of August, he sent some bad news to the general: eleven British vessels had sailed up a branch of the Santee "to carry off rice, eight hundred barrels (of which) Lay on that Branch." He added that he had removed some of the rice and some military stores to a safe place, but that a considerable quantity of rice had fallen into the enemy's hand.

Early in September, Marion found himself engaged in an enterprise that involved higher stakes than the defense of stocks of corn, rice, or salt. General Greene, having given his troops several weeks to rest and regain their health, had decided to descend from the high hill of Santee with the hope of surprising the British army. Since his Continentals were outnumbered by the British regulars, who were under the command of Lieutenant-Colonel Alexander Stewart, he was obliged to incorporate Marion's brigade of irregulars into his field army. So the Swamp Fox found himself committed to the line of battle in case of a collision with Stewart's redcoats. Even as he marched to battle, however, he pursued his usual role of intelligence officer. He and Henry Lee were sent riding ahead of Greene's army to screen its advance. Their mission was twofold: they were to detain the inhabitants of the Santee River valley so they would be unable to warn Stewart of the approach of the strength in troops and artillery.

Marion and Lee performed their duties well. They prevented loyalists from warning Stewart of Greene's approach, and they found the British camp. Having found it, Marion promptly wrote to his superior that "the Enemy is at Eutaw. They sent two Detachments to Monks Corner, one Yesterday and the other the day before." Unfortunately, he was unable to furnish Greene with an exact account of British troop strength, but the general was able to find out for himself when he advanced close to his adversary's camp and surprised and captured a large number of foragers.

After his initial success against the British foraging party, Greene advanced upon Stewart's post at Eutaw Springs. His army had a slight numerical superiority over the British, but the advantage of surprise was lost to it because some dragoons who had fled from the preliminary skirmish warned Stewart of its advance. Thanks to the warning, the British were able to form a line of battle in time to defend their camp. But the Americans, with Marion's militia fighting in the front line, drove the redcoats from their camp in confusion. Yet the British were not driven from the field. Rallying after they had seemingly been beaten, they made a tenacious defense of a brick plantation house and of the fence and outbuilding which surrounded it. Greene's Maryland and Virginia Continentals attempted to storm the house, but they were beaten off with heavy losses.

Unable to drive the British from the plantation house, Greene was finally obliged to order his troops to retreat. "Nothing," he wrote after the action, "but the brick house and the peculiar strength of the position at Eutaw saved the British Army from being all made Prisoners." Although he had been unable to win a decisive victory, he had the satisfaction of knowing that his troops had taken many prisoners. As evidence that he had won a victory after all, he learned that Stewart had evacuated the battlefield shortly after the action.

Marion was as disappointed as was Greene. His militia had fought gallantly and had suffered the loss of many officers and men killed or wounded. Yet their sacrifices had been rewarded by something less than a decisive victory. Nevertheless, as both Greene and Marion were soon to discover, the battle had broken the aggressiveness of the British army. The British did not take the offensive again; on the contrary, they confined themselves to the defense of Charleston and the farms and plantations located within thirty miles of it.

Shortly after the battle, Marion turned anew to his intelligence gathering. He sent Hezekiah Maham, who had been promoted from major to lieutenant colonel, to reconnoiter the British post at Monck's Corner. At the same time, he attempted to intercept six supply schooners, which were plying the Santee escorted by an armed galley. His plans for capturing the schooners went away because some Negroes who had hoped for rewards from the British "gave the enemy intelligence of our position," but his efforts to learn of enemy movements and troop strength continued to prosper. Indeed his intelligence work was facilitated by the demoralization which set in among the British after Eutaw Springs. Many deserters and stragglers were picked up by Marion's patrols during the fall of 1781 and the winter that followed. Thus, information about the British army became readily available, and Marion and his officers were able to corroborate evidence furnished by one prisoner or deserter by questioning others and by scouting enemy post as Mahan had done at Moncks Corner.

During the fall and winter additional sources of information became available to Marion and Greene. Their patrols were able to advance to within a few miles of Charleston, and they were able to question civilians whom the British allowed to leave town to attend to business on their plantations. Such informants often volunteered misleading information; however, and it was necessary for Marion to verify their accounts by consulting other sources. Marion's sources included his own scouts, British deserters and prisoners, and a Charlestonian whom he had engaged to act as a spy. That he had an agent working for him is clear from the following passage in one of his letters to Greene: "A letter from Charleston says there is net two months provisions in town. This Letter is from a man in my employment."

By the end of 1781, Marion had become highly competent as an intelligence officer. He had long since learned to distinguish between hearsay and eyewitness accounts, and he had discovered that information learned from experience to corroborate evidence from such sources. For example, he learned toward the end of 1781, from a woman who had just left Charleston, that Major-General Alexander Leslie had arrived there to take command of the British army in the Lower South. It was true that Leslie had arrived and had assumed command of all British troops in South Carolina and Georgia. But the woman volunteered that Leslie had landed together with a number of troops; indeed she claimed that she had seen them "but could not tell how many." How exasperating such vague information must have been to Marion! He and Greene needed to know if reinforcements had landed at Charleston, and if so, how many troops and guns were included in it.

Marion forwarded the lady's story to Greene, but he was careful to make clear in his letter that her information was fuzzy. She could have mistaken troops who had paraded to welcome Leslie for newly arrived troops, but just in case redcoats had landed, Marion warned Greene that a reinforcement might have arrived. Having done so, he turned his efforts to ascertaining the facts about the alleged reinforcement. Soon he was able to report, probably on the basis of information from his agent in Charleston, that: "I have certain Intelligence of General Lesleys coming to town but with only a staff of six men."

During the winter of 1781–1782 Marion's work was made easier for him because large numbers of British soldiers and South Carolina loyalists deserted or defected. In early January, 1782, Marion reported to his superior that "I have had twenty Deserters come to me within these eight Days." The twenty deserters and other who followed them brought with them a steady flow of information. But they brought more than information; many of them brought rumors thatwere unfounded, but Marion allowed himself to be taken in by them. He had learned from experience that rumors were likely to be unreliable or completely false, but his guard was down because of the optimism induced by the news that Lord Cornwallis's army had surrendered to a combined Franco-American force of Yorktown, Virginia. Having been lulled into wishful thinking as result of the news from Yorktown, he made one of his false reports to Greene when he said months too soon that "every intelligence from Charlestown indicates an evacuation of that town taking place."

Marion's premature reports of the evacuation of Charlestown was one of his few mistakes as an intelligence officer. His mistake had been more than offset, however, by his success in reporting the march of General Leslie's redcoats from Charleston to Winnsboro and of Lord Rawdon's relief column from the low country to the beleaguered fort at Ninety Six. Moreover, he had reported accurately upon the strength and armament of numerous British garrisons and detachments. And he had been correct when he had informed Greene, at the end of 1781 that Leslie had returned to South Carolina but had brought no troops with him.

In evaluating Marion's success as an intelligence officer it should be pointed out that Greene's army was never surprised by Cornwallis or Rawdon. Both sides attempted to achieve the advantage of surprise from time to time, but the only army which was taken by surprise was,thanks to the sealing of the countryside around Eutaw Springs by Lee and Marion,the British one commanded by Colonel Stewart.

From *Swamp Fox* by Robert Bass, Sandlapper Publishing Company:

In September 1780, Francis Marion was encamped at Port's Ferry where, among the ardent Whigs of Britton's Neck, he was relatively secure. While he waited there for Peter Horry to join him, Francis Goddard and his half-brothers Samuel and Britton Jenkins, sons of the Revolutionary War heroine the Window Jenkins, joined his little band.

As partisan warfare raged across the countryside of eastern South Carolina, it was hard to know who was on which side of the conflict. Some families included both Whigs and Tories, and many simply switched sides based on which militia was passing through. Stories of individuals who stood up to the British and Loyalist forces spread rapidly and were a source of encouragement for the hard-pressed Whigs. Elizabeth Jenkins, a prominent plantation owner in Britton's Neck, provided more than one such story.

In March 1781, with Greene and Cornwallis in North Carolina and Sumter retreating to the Backcountry, Lt. Col. Francis, Lord Rawdon, the British commanding officer at Camden, devised a pincer plan to defeat Francis Marion and the Whigs forces in the northeastern corner of South Carolina. Rawdon diverted Col. Welbore Ellis Doyle and the Volunteers of Ireland from Camden to attack Marion's Snow's Island camp. At the same time, he sent Col. John Watson and a combined British Loyalist to find Marion, who was in hiding near Murray's Ferry on the Santee River. For the next three weeks, Marion conducted a slow tactical retreat towards Georgetown, harassing Watson along the way. By the time Watson and his men, reached the Sampit River, it was all they could do to make it to the safety of the British-occupied port.

During the fierce chase, Marion and his opponents also engaged in a fierce war of words over the exchange of prisoners. One of Marion's officers, Capt. John Postell, was captured while delivering British prisoners to Georgetown. Although riding under a flag of truce, Postell had violated the terms of a British parole by rejoining the Whigs forces. Furious that the British commandant in Georgetown, Capt. John Saunders, had violated Postell's white flag,

Marion appealed to Lt. Col. Nisbet Balfour in Charleston, the senior British officer in the province. Balfour balked. Instead of returning Postell he sent the original parole, the evidence of Postell's offense; and a curt reply to Saunders for delivery to Marion, advising him "to be careful who you send; a non-commissioned officer will be best, for fear (Marion) detains the person sent on account of Postell.

Rather than heed Balfour's advice, Saunders sent Cornet Thomas Merritt, a junior officer, to deliver the letter. In uniform and bearing a white flag, Merritt rode off to find Marion's Snow's Island camp. At Britton's Neck the two stopped at the plantation of Elizabeth Jenkins, the ferryman's cousin. Not realizing that Merritt was a Tory, his green uniform resembled those of the Continental troops under Light Horse Harry Lee, Jenkins asked her cousin if it would be safe for her sixteen-year-old son James to go down to buy salt in Waccamaw Neck, an area of Whig sympathizers just north of Georgetown.

"No, madam," interjected Merritt, "for we have a great big thing there we call a galley."

Jenkins did not take kindly to Merritt's condescension. Though she lived in relative isolation away from the port cities of the coast, Jenkins was a woman of culture who had attended school in Charleston as a girl. "Sir, I suppose you think you have got so far back in the country that no one here ever saw a galley but you," she snapped. "I'll have you know, sir, that I have been as well raised as yourself."

Clearly unwelcome, the visitors prepared to leave. Turning on the ferryman, she said, "Cousin Britton, if you cannot bring any better company with you than this, you'd better keep away." And she slammed the door behind them.

When the two arrived at Marion's redoubt at Dunham's Bluff, Col. Hugh Ervin took Merritt prisoner, insurance against any British mistreatment of Postell.

By late March, bested by Marion's guerilla tactics and suffering serious casualties, Watson had no choice but to retreat across the Sampit River to Georgetown. Safely back in British-controlled territory, he complained of Marion and his men: "They will not sleep and fight like gentlemen, but like savages are eternally firing and whooping around us by night, and by day waylaying and popping at us from behind every tree!"

Determined to pursue his opponent, Watson rested his men only a short while, and in early April they set out again. Passing through lower Prince Frederick Parish (today northeastern Williamsburg), they crossed the Pee Dee at Britton's Ferry. About 9 o'clock on the morning of April 7 Watson and his men reached the home of Elizabeth Jenkins. The soldiers camped in her dry sandy field, and during the day Watson used the house for his headquarters. Defenseless, Jenkins had a little choice but to give the British what they wanted. While both feigned courtesy, Jenkins and her unwelcome guest could not help attempting to get the best of each other through verbal jabs. She asked Watson if he had any difficulty getting from the ferry to her place, as Marion's men had torn up the bridges.

"No, madam, I never find a difficulty when on British ground. Do you not believe, madam, the British will conquer the Americans?"

Watson flushed angrily. "No, madam, I do not believe it," he replied. "How many sons have you among the rebels, madam?"

"None, sir" she said. "The king has rebelled against us, and not we against the king."

"Well, madam, how many sons have you with Marion?"

"I have three, sir," she replied. Francis Goddard, her son by her first marriage, and Samuel and Britton Jenkins, sons by her second, all served under Marion. "I only wish they were three thousand."

"Send for them, madam," Watson pleaded. "Let them take protecting, marry wives, and settle their plantations."

"Will you stay, sir and protect them?"

"No, Madam, indeed," he replied, confident in British victory. "It is enough for me to pardon them."

"Pardon them, sir!" she retorted. "They have not asked it yet."

Exasperated, he asked her to have a glass of wine with him. As he raised his glass, he cried: "Health to King George!"

Jenkins politely drank the toast and refilled the glasses. As he raised his glass again, she cried: "Health to George Washington!"

Watson made a wry face, but, being a gentlemen, he cheerfully toasted the commander of the Continentals. He then tried a gambit. "Well, madam, have you heard that General Marion has joined Lord Rawdon?"

"No, sir, indeed I have not," she retorted, knowing that her nephew had seen Marion the previous day.

"Well, madam," he insisted, it is a matter of fact."

"Sir, I don't believe it."

"Why, madam, you might as well tell me I lie."

"I don't say you lie, sir," she said with a smile, "but I don't believe it."

Watson was so vexed with his unwilling hostess that he moved his men a mile across the sand fields and camped at John Rae's for the night.

But the soldiers left their mark on the Jenkins plantation Jenkins' youngest son, sixteen-year-old James, had spent the day with his cousin, John Jenkins, whom Colonel Peter Horry had sent to scout Watson's advance. When James returned after nightfall, he found the place plundered of provisions. "Upon my return home," he wrote in his autobiography, "I found that they had made sad havoc among the beeves and beef, having killed no less than seven, which they skinned and left on the spot, because too poor for them. The garden was almost entirely destroyed those hungry soldiers."

Northeast on Catfish Creek, along Little Pee Dee and up the Branches of Drowning Creek were many people who felt they had little in common with the Low Country and were still loyal to the King of England. They had formed a regiment of Loyalist militia under the command of Major Micajah Ganey, with Jesse Barefield as second in command. Allied with British invaders, these Tories were as dangerous as the redcoats themselves. Receiving word that Marion was camping at Port's Ferry, Ganey called out his militia - 250 men – to the mustering field on Little PeeDee. Since Marion kept his scouts moving and listing, he was not to be caught by surprise. With only 52 men, however, what should be his course of action?

He rejected the idea of running and decided to attack first. Before daylight on September 4, Marion was up and riding from

Port's Ferry to surprise the Tories who were up and preparing to surprise him at Port's Ferry. His Brigade first scattered Ganey's horsemen and them pursued the Tory infantry under Barefield into the Blue Savannah morass. In these two skirmishes, at a cost of four men wounded and two horses killed, he broke the power of the Tories east of the Pee Dee.

Almost immediately afterwards, sixty volunteers rode into his camp, and with his forces doubled, Marion began to fortify his retreat. To protect the Ferry, "awe the Tories," and blockade the post road that ran from Savannah to Boston, he threw up a redoubt of logs and clay and behind the ramparts mounted two small cannon. They pointed along the road and across the river as guardians of the area's liberty and freedom.

When Lord Rawden evacuated Camden, on May 10, 1781, Harrison followed him to Charlestown. He was stationed at the Quarter House on Charlestown Neck. During the next six months, the South Carolina Rangers served as barrack troops. Their morale began to droop. In eighteen months of service their regiment had suffered 42 percent loss in dead, wounded, missing, and deserted. It is axiomatic that when a military corps suffers a loss of more than 10 percent, it loses its élan, its fighting ability.

The glory and the hope had passed. The Muster Master Rigdon Brice held his muster and inspection on December 24, 1781; the enlistments of the South Carolina Rangers expired. No-one would reenlist. John Harrison lowered his flag in defeat and resigned his commission as major. The next day he accepted a commission as captain and Sam Harrison accepted one as lieutenant. About a dozen veterans followed them into a troop of South Carolina Dragoons.

When the British evacuated Charlestown on December 14, 1782, they shipped Harrison and his troops to St. Augustine. There, he and his men transferred to the infantry of Fraser's South Carolina Royalists. They remained until the signing of the treaty of peace between the United States and Great Britain. In their final muster there were two commissioned officers, two noncommissioned officers, and nine privates of the original South Carolina Rangers.

In his usual blend of fact and fiction, Judge James wrote, "During the contest, the major was killed; after it was over, the colonel retired to Jamaica with much wealth acquired by depredations."

James was wrong. John Harrison was never promoted to colonel, and Sam was never promoted to major. They had served their king valiantly, and they retired on half – pay at their final rank. According to the half – pay records in the Public Records Office in London, John lived until 1795. Although in *Swamp Fox*, this writer, following James, killed Sam off at Wiboo Swamp, he survived to enjoy his half pay until 1816.

The Swamp Fox Earns His Name

From *Swamp Fox* by Robert Bass, Sandlapper Publishing Company:

Banastre Tarleton, sometimes called "Bloody Tarleton," was a brutal and ruthless British officer who led a large unit of mounted soldiers known as the Green Dragoons or Green Horse. This unit was both highly effective militarily and infamous for their brutality. On the night of November 7, 1780, Tarleton and his legion along with a large group of Tories (Americana loyal to the British king) called Harrison's Provincials had camped at the Widow Richardson's plantation hoping to surprise and destroy Francis Marion's smaller forces. WidowRichardson, however, sent her son to warn Marion of Tarleton's trap.

Marion knew it would be foolhardy to fight Tarleton's large, well trained, and well armed force in any kind of pitched battle, and he certainly did not wish to have his militia ambushed. Upon being warned, Marion reversed his direction in the dark of the night, skirted Woodyard Swamp, and galloped across Richbourg's Mill Dam on Jack's Creek. However, in their haste to extricate themselves from Tarleton's trap. Marion's militia allowed a Tory prisoner to escape. This escaped prisoner reached Tarleton just before dawn on November 8. By daybreak Harrison's Provincials and the Green Horse were moving at a gallop down the road to Richbourg's Mill Dam in hot pursuit of Marion's militia.

Being as wily as Tarleton, Marion realized when he reversed direction that Tarleton would soon find out that the British trap had failed. Tarleton's brutal Green Dragoons and Harrison's Provincials would be angry and would spare neither horses nor men to catch and annihilate the Williamsburg Militia. Speed and guile were the Patriot's best friends in the hours before dawn on November 8, 1780. In the early hours before dawn, Marion's men were moving swiftly through the great pine barrens which separate the Santee and Black Rivers, guided by militiamen who knew this wilderness. Major James formed a rear guard and Marion led, letting Ball (his horse captured from the British) run as fast as he would.

From Richbourg's Mill, the militia galloped toward the headwaters of Jack's Creek and made a rapid turn down the Pocotaligo River. Ball set a blistering pace with the other horses following just behind. Until early afternoon the Patriots sped along back roads which were little more than paths, across barren fields, through the dark pine woods, and across boggy and forbidding swamps. Following the Pocotaligo, ready to swim the river should Tarleton overtake him, Marion finally emerged from the vast wilderness to find the familiar roads close to the Black River. He slowed the pace and at Benbow's Ferry the horses walked into the cold dark waters of the Black River and crossed over.

For seven hours, covering twenty-six miles without stopping, through swamps, forests, fields, and trackless pine barren the Green Dragoons and Harrison's Provincials chased Marion. Finally at Ox Swamp, about twenty-three miles north of Kingstree, they halted at the beginning of a roadless bog. The dragoons and provincials were tired and hungry, their horses exhausted. Tarleton reigned in his horse and addressing his troops said, "Come my boys! Let us go back, and we will find the Gamecock (Thomas Sumter). But as for this----(expletive deleted) old fox, the devil himself could not catch him!" Tarleton's quote became famous among both Tories and Whigs (Patriots) and soon the nickname "Swamp Fox" was forever attached to the wily little man who so brilliantly led his militia band out of Tarleton's trap. Marion would go on to fight many times but would never be caught or captured by any British or Tory militia unit, and would gain a measure of immortality as the "Swamp Fox."

The Sharpshooters

In the Revolutionary War in the South, the firearm used by the British was the musket. It fired a large projectile but was accurate for only about fifty yards. There was no spiral grooves on the inside of the barrel to make the projectile spin in flight. A spinning projectile will go relatively straight for a much greater distance than a projectile which does not spin. To overcome the disadvantages of inaccuracy of their muskets, the British used large numbers of troops firing in a line to achieve a "shotgun" effect with muskets. Even if the infantryman firing the musket did not hit the enemy soldier at whom his musket was pointed, he might very well hit another enemy soldier in the opposing line of enemy troops. Two large opposing forces fired at relatively close range into a line of enemy troops. The British would often follow the musket fire with a bayonet charge. The British were very well trained with the bayonet and excelled in this type of close quartered combat.

The warfare practiced by Francis Marion took away some of the advantage of this massed British firepower. Marion's men would fire from concealed positions or from behind tree trunks, ditches, or other structures making them much harder to hit with the muskets (or rifle cannon fire for that matter).

Some of Marion's men used a relatively new invention, the rifle. Others used muskets loaded with buckshot, swan-shot, or single projectiles. The rifle had spiral grooves cut into the inside of the barrel (as described above) to impart a spin to the projectile, resulting in a straighter flight over much longer distances. Some of Captain William McCottry's riflemen (Williamsburg militia under command of Francis Marion) could consistently hit targets up to three hundred yards distant, whereas muskets were not generally accurate for more than fifty yards. The rifles and ammunition of Marion's day were primitive in their design and manufactured with the rifles having only simple iron sights as opposed to the sophisticated telescopic sights available today. The skill and effectiveness of some of the backwoods sharpshooters awed and terrorized the British. Coupled with mobility (good horses), knowledge of geography and terrain (where to set an ambush), guerrilla tactics, and innovations such as Maham Tower, the sharpshooters helped the Patriots overcome the British advantage in numbers, equipment, training, and firepower.

Port's Ferry overlooked Britton's Neck. Northeast on Catfish Creek, along Little Pee Dee and up the branches of Drowning Creek were many people who, feeling they had little in common with the Low-country, were still loyal to the King of England. They had formed a regiment of Loyalists militia under the command of Major Micajah Ganey, with Captain Jesse Barefield as second in command. Allied with the British invaders, they burned, looted, fought and killed. The Battle of Port's Ferry occurred on September 5, when Major Ganey, having received notice that Marion was camping at Port's Ferry, called out his militia to the mustering field on Little Pee Dee and set out to surprise the rebels. When Marion's scouts notified him of the development, he considered his options. "What could he do with only fifty-two men? He could run and forfeit forever the trust of his patriots. He could await Ganey's attack and then fight him behind every gut and slough in Britton's Neck. Or, he could attack first."

He was up before day on September 4. So that his men might distinguish each other from the Tories, since all wore homespun, he ordered them to mount white cockades on their caps.

Marion himself reported to his commanding general: "On the third instant I had advice that upwards of two hundred Tories intended to attack me the next day. I immediately marched with fifty-two men, which is all I could get on the fourth in the morning, and surprised a party of forty-five men, who escaped. I then marched immediately, to attack the main body, whom I met about three miles in full march towards me. I directly attacked them to flight (though they had two hundred men) and got into an impassable swamp (the Blue Savannah) to all but Tories.

Wemyss's Foray and the Hanging of Adam Cusack

In their efforts to pacify the Carolina backcountry, the harsh tactics of the British often had the opposite of their desired effect. Bitterness and anger rose. More families took up arms against the King, and stories of British atrocities became grits for the Whig propaganda mill. The foray of Major James Wemyss and his Sixty-Third Regiment into the area between the Santee and Pee Dee in August and September 1780 provides one example of their failed strategy and its life in local lore.

Marion's victories at Sumter's house and the Blue Savannah in August 1780, first surprised, then angered the British. To protect Georgetown, the anchor of their flank, Col. Balfour called in British regulars and Loyalist militias as reinforcements and ordered improvements to the seaport's defenses.

Disarm in the Most Rigid Manner

Lord Cornwallis also acted swiftly. He knew that a victorious band of guerillas astride the long supply line between Camden and Charleston would be fatal. As soon as he learned of Marion's strike at Sumter's house, he ordered Major James Wemyss to march the Sixty-Third Regiment from the High Hills to Kingstree. "I should advise your sweeping the country entirely from Kingstree Bridge to Peedee, and returning by the Cheraws," he wrote on August 28. "I would have you disarm in the most rigid manner, all Persons who cannot be depended on and punish the concealment of Arms and ammunition with a total demolition of the plantation." Without exact knowledge of Marion's strength, but knowing the Sixty-Third Regiment was weak from malaria, Cornwallis ordered all available Loyalist forces to cooperate in the movement.

According to legend, facing a march of 150 miles, Wemyss decided to mount his regiment. Calling together all the Whig planters in the High Hills, he lectured them for an hour while troops scoured the area, rounding up their horses. When the planters discovered the rustling, they protested vigorously, but in vain. The horses were in British corals and heavily guarded. "The enraged countrymen walked home," said David Ramsay, "but soon after many of them repaired to General Marion."

As Wemyss marched toward Kingstree, Marion's men captured and questioned a member of his rear guard. Learning of the movementof Wemyss's men and the other British and Loyalist units, Marion realized his sixty men were facing some thousand or fifteen hundred adversaries. Rather than fight against impossible odds, he chose to retreat into North Carolina.

In Willamsburg, meanwhile, Major Wemyss and Captain Amos Gaskens, a local Loyalist, were attempting to disable the rebel movement, targeting the home of Whig militiamen. However, personal and church records indicate that Wemyss himself, like most Scout of his day, was a lifelong Presbyterian.

At the home of Major John James, one of Marion's officers, he held Mrs. James and her children hostage for two days, hoping that Major James would come to his family. The father failed to appear, but Wemyss sent a patrol to the home of Captain John James, his son, to take him into custody. The younger James had been on patrol after the fall of Charleston, but he taken up arms back home in Williamsburg. He was so outraged at the treatment of his mother and siblings that had fired on a small party of Tories raiding McGill's plantation. "If he is found to have broken his parole," the Major swore, "he will be hanged in the morning to yonder tree!"

The next morning Wemyss held an impromptu court-martial. Neither member of the James families nor their slaves could or would testify. Wemyss was forced to release them all, but he burned the house of the James in retaliation. William Dobein James, another son who at age fifteen was among Marion's men (and would go on to author one of the most valuable accounts of the general's career), wrote later of the consequences of the arson: "I felt an early inclination to record these events; but Major Wemyss burnt all my stock of paper, and my little classical library, in my father's house and, for two years and a half afterward, I had not the common implements of writing or of reading."

Under the guidance of local Tories, Wemyss's men burned a swath fifteen miles wide along the seventy-mile route from Kingstree to Cheraw. Believing that the way to suppress the rebellion was to hand the leaders and destroy the resources of the rebels, he ordered his men to break up the looms, fire the grist mills, and destroy the blacksmith shops. To deprive the Whigs of the means of existence, he had his troops shoot milk cows and bayonet sheep. At the same time, Marion's men were exacting similar punishment on Loyalist homes. In a report to Cornwallis, he said that the rebels were "burning houses, and distressing the well-affected in a most severe manner. Several people from that Country have been with me to represent their distressed Situation. The highlanders in particular who are very numerous here, have been treated with such Cruelty & Oppression as almost exceeds belief." In the fall of 1780, the bitter civil war in the South Carolina backcountry touched many families on both sides of the political divide.

The Hanging of Adam Cusack

Wemyss certainly targeted the homes of Whig leaders and militiamen and sought to punish those who defied the British. According to local lore, one such Whig supporter was Adam Cusack, who had been paroled at Charleston and returned to his home. Cusack had refused to ferry some British officers across Black Creek. Resentful, he later shot across the creek at a slave of Captain John Brockington, a Tory from Kingstree, and missed. Wemyss ordered his arrest. Cusack was tried in a court-martial, found guilty of breaking his parole by resorting to firearms, and sentenced to death. Wemyss ordered a scaffold build beside the road at Long Bluff and personally supervised the execution. William Dobein James recounts that Cusack's "wife and children prostrated themselves before Wemyss, on horseback, for a pardon; and he would have rode over them, had not one of his own officers prevented the foul deed." Just before the soldiers tripped the platform under the prisoner, James Wilson, a local physician, attempted to intercede. As punishment for this officer, Wemyss later destroyed much of Wilson's property and burned his home. After his wife sought safety in North Carolina, Wilson joined Marion's band.

Some of the dramatic details of the story as recorded by James may have been added for Whig propaganda purpose. Shortly after the publication of James's book, Wemyss made his own statement about the Cusack incident from his home on Long Island, New York: "Although much property was destroyed in the execution of the above orders [i.e. his August 28 orders from Cornwallis], it ever affords Colonel Wemyss the greatest satisfaction on reflecting that one man only suffered death. He was a native of England, and formerly a boatswains mate in a British Man of War, from which he had deserted, and was particularly distinguished for cruelty and persecution of every Loyalist in that part of the Country. The day before he was taken, he attempted to kill an officer of the Loyal Militia on his way to join Colonel Wemyss's detachment, and took from him a valuable horse."

On September 20, Wemyss reported to Lord Cornwallis from Cheraw: "I have done everything in my Power to get at Mr. Marion, who with Giles commanded about 150 Men on my arrival in this part of the Country. Although I never could come up with them, yet I pushed them so hard as in a great measure to break them up; the few that still continued together have retreated over Little Pee Dee." Surveying the state of the rebellion in the district between the Santee and the Pee Dee, he stated that almost every family was involved. He added that he had "burnt and laid waste about 50 houses and Plantations, mostly belonging to People who have either broke their Paroles or Oaths of Allegiance, and are now in Arms against us." Wemyss admitted that his activities had won few friends for Great Britain. He told his commander that the area "cannot be kept by militia," but would instead need regular troops to control the rebellion. Cornwallis, assessing the negative impact of Wemyss's foray, confided to an associate: "I am much disappointed in that business."

"I had one man wounded in the first action and three in the second and two horses killed." The next day, eighty volunteers rode into his camp.

Marion then fortified his retreat. To protect the ferry and blockade the post road he had a redoubt of logs and mud thrown up on the eastern bank of the Pee Dee and behind the rampart mounted two small cannon to command both the road and the river.

Like most of the 160 military engagements of this period, Port's Ferry and Blue Savannah were minor ones; however they had the significant effect of breaking the power of the Tories east of the Pee Dee.

Retreat is not normally a word associated with victory, but the story of Apple Cider and Peter Horry's is an exception. Colonel Peter Horry was Marion's second in command and an experienced militia leader. British Major McLeroth and his troops were moving back toward Kingstree from Nelson's Ferry when Francis Marion caught wind of McLeroth's position. It was rumored that Colonel Tynes, a Loyalist militia leader had come out of hiding with his militia and was going to be fighting alongside McLeroth's troops, making their force even stronger and became formidable foes. Marion rounded up his troops and set out to find the British.

Marion's force stopped off in Indian Town briefly to devise a strategy and "the proper precautions against surprise." Peter Horry's troops broke off to go through the High Hills of Santee (west of present day Sumter) to scout Colonel Tyne's new post located at Fort Upton. Horry's men rode through the night along a road east of Black River. In the morning they made a stop at a tavern whose owner was known for having sympathy toward the loyalist (pro-British) and Horry's men treated the tavern owner "with the rough attention they felt on account of his political persuasion." After finishing lunch Horry began to question the tavern keeper. Meanwhile the cleaver tavern keeper's wife led one of Horry's men to a shed out back; she silently pointed to a barrel of apple cider brandy, of which the soldier began immediately to partake. He then called over some of the other soldiers. They all enjoyed several rounds in addition to filling their canteens to the brim for later enjoyment.

As the men set off again Horry began to notice that his troops were oddly giddy and constantly sipping from their canteens. The good Colonel asked them what they were drinking to which they replied, "Water, sir, nothing but water!" Horry knew this was a bold-face lie, as he said later that "some grinned in my face like monkeys: others looked as stupid as asses; while others chattered like magpies." All of the troops were extremely inebriated except for Captain Nelson and Peter Horry, of course.

Colonel Horry's guide, "a jolter-headed fellow who was possessed of a great belly, lurched back and forth in such magnificent sweeps that he finally lost his balance and toppled to the ground, a limp and sodden mass of drunken blubber." There was no point in continuing the mission; their cries created such a ruckus that it would have been impossible to sneak up on a deaf man. The forest reverberated with the sound of their revelry and they were totally incapable of fighting a battle. Horry had no course but to retreat. Their retreat was executed "with all the irregularity that might have been expected from a troop of drunkards, each of whom mistaking himself for commander-in-chief, gave orders according to his own mad humor; and whopped and hallooed at such a rate, that I verily believe no bull drivers ever made half the racket."

Horry's intoxicated troops returned to camp. A dejected Horry made his report to Marion about their alcohol retreat. Upon hearing the story, Marion let a "rare chuckle escape his lips." Marion commended Horry on making the right decision under the circumstances and "slyly added, 'But pray keep a careful eye on the apple water next time."

It may seem as though the patrol to scout and possibly attack Fort Upton failed when the entire activity devolved into a drunken circus. However, Lady Fortune smiled on Peter Horry and the Patriots that day. Horry's drunken troops created such a clamor with their inebriated shenanigans that the Black River Loyalists, in a state of alarm, spread word that Marion's troops were in the area. By the time this story had reached Upton Hill, it became so exaggerated that it was said General Harrington's entire command (patriots) was marching to attack Fort Upton. Only twenty of Tynes Loyalist militia stayed with him; the rest fled upon hearing this story. This impressive loss of troops frightened Tynes into leaving Fort Upton and begging for permission to resign as militia leader. His resignation was accepted.

The outcome of a battle, if one had occurred, would not have had such a favorable outcome for Marion's troops. There would have been dead and wounded. Instead, the troops had only to worry about their colossal hangover. The actual results of this little misadventure were far more beneficial for Marion and the patriots than anyone could have imagined. Ironically, a large quantity of Loyalist apple cider and a consequent drunken retreat resulted in one of the oddest victories of the Revolutionary War and a number of lives on both sides were probably speared.

After the battle of Sullivan's Island in 1776, which drove the British out of Charleston harbor, Marion was promoted to Lieutenant Colonel. He spent the next three years on duty around Charleston, and then in 1779 he commanded his regiment in an unsuccessful assault on Savannah, where his troops suffered high casualties. In May 1780, the British returned in force and captured Charleston, but they didn't get Marion, thanks to an odd event. Two months earlier, Marion, a teetotaler, decided to leave a regimental party which became a drinking bout. Undeterred by the host locking the party-goers in, Marion jumped from a second-floor window. When Charleston's Continental garrison surrendered to the British, Marion was at his plantation recuperating from a sprained ankle and thus escaped capture.

Charleston had fallen in the battle on May 12, 1780, and the citizens of Williamsburg, many of whose sons had served in the siege of that city, decided "something must be done." Just before that time, John James had been sent from Charleston to Williamsburg to organize the district into a fighting force. They decided to send Captain John James. He interviewed the British commander at Georgetown in order to ascertain just what would be expected of the people of Williamsburg. The British commander shouted, "I shall require unqualified submission from them; and, as for you, I shall have you hanged!" The British commander drew his sword, which Captain James parried with a chair. In a moment, Captain James had escaped and mounted the coal – black charger "Thunder," and that war horse was moving towards Williamsburg! Captain James reached The King's Tree (a sturdy oak that was located, moved, and planted in the name of King Charles) that night. The word reached every corner of the territory within three days. Men began to gather at King's Tree and formed a battalion and elected John James "Major." This group became important as Marion's Brigade. This incident began the War of the Revolution. Major James and Captain Mouzon knew Lieutenant Colonel Francis Marion. They had been close to him under fire. He did not talk much; he did things. Williamsburg District called Francis Marion to command, and he came. No man ever commanded several Scotch companies with greater success than this "silent man." The officers and men flocked about General Marion to obtain a sight of their future commander, who was rather of bold and middle stature, lean and wiry. His body was well set, but his knees and ankles were badly formed, and he still limped upon one leg.

The history of the American Revolution is a history of miracles, all calling out to us: America will be free!

Marion with God's help was that man that set us free. It was he who, with his feeble force, dared to dash up at once to Nelson's Ferry on the great warpath between British armies at Charleston and Camden.

"Now, my gallant friends," said he, at sight of the road, and with a face burning for battle, "now look sharp! Here are the British wagon tracks, with the sand still falling in and here are the steps of their troops passing. We shall not long be idle here!"

And so it turned out. For scarcely had we reached our hiding place in Snow's Island Swamp, in came our scouts at half-speed, stating that a British guard, with a world of American prisoners, were on their march to Charleston.

"How many prisoners do you suppose there were?" said Marion.
"Near two hundred," replied the scouts.
"And what do you imagine was the number of British Guard?"
"Why, sir, we counted about ninety."

"Ninety!" said Marion with a smile. "Ninety! Well, that will do. And now, gentlemen, if you will only stand by me, I've a good hope that we will have those ninety by tomorrow's sunrise."

Lead on, for that he was resolved to die or to conquer. As soon as the dusky night came on, we went down to the ferry, and passing for a party of good Loyalists, we easily got set over. The enemy, with their prisoners, having just affected the passage of the river as the sun went down, halted at the first tavern, generally called "the Blue House" where the officers ordered supper. In front of the building was a large arbor, wherein the toppers were wont to die, and spend the jocund night away in songs and gleeful draughts of apple brandy grog. In this arbor, flushed with their late success, sat the British guard, singing away to the tune of "Brittannia Strike Home" until overcome with fatigue and liquor, and down they sunk to the ground.

Just as they called this last born day, we approached the house in perfect concealment behind a string of fence within a few yards of it. In spite of all our address, we could not effect a complete surprise of them. Their sentinels took the alarm, and firing their pieces, they fled into the yard. Swift as lightening, we entered with them, and seizing their muskets, which were all stacked near the gate, we made prisoners of the whole party, without having been obliged to kill more than three of them.

After securing their arms, Marion called for their captain, but he was not to be found high or low, among the living or dead. However, after a hot search, he was found up the chimney! He begged very hard that we not let his men know where he had concealed himself. Nothing could equal the mortification of the British when they came to see that a handful of militia men had taken them and recovered all of their prisoners.

Marion had high hopes that the American regulars, whom he had so gallantly rescued, would have joined his arms and fought hard to avenge their late defeat. However, equally to his surprise and their own disgrace, not one of them could be prevailed on to shoulder a musket! "Where is the use," said they, "of fighting now when all is lost?"

This was the general impression. Except for these unconquerable spirits, Marion and Sumter, with a few of the same heroic stamp who kept the field, Carolina was no better than a British province.

In our late attack on the enemy, we had but four rounds of powder and ball and not a single sword that deserved the name, but Marion soon remedied the defect. He bought up all of the old saw blades from the mills and gave them to the smith, who presently manufactured for us a parcel of substantial broadswords, sufficient, as I have often seen, to kill a man at a single blow.

From our prisoners in the late action, we were completely armed. Armed with a couple of English muskets, with bayonets and cartouche boxes, for each of us, we retreated into Britton's Neck.

We had not been there above twenty four hours before news was brought to us by a trusty friend that the Tories, on Pee Dee, were mustering, in force, under a Captain Barfield. We were quickly on horseback and after a brisk ride of forty miles, came upon their encampment at three o'clock in the morning. Their surprise was so complete that they did not fire a single shot! Of the forty-nine men who composed their company we killed and took about thirty. The arms, ammunition, and horses of the whole party fell into our hands, with which we returned to Britton's Neck, without the loss of a man.

The rumor of these exploits soon reached the British and their friends, the Tories, who presently dispatched three stout companies to attack us. Two of the parties were British, one of them commanded by Major Weymies, of house – burning memory. The third party was altogether Tories. We fled before them towards North Carolina. Supposing they had entirely scouted us, they gave over the chase and retreated to their respective stations: the British to Georgetown and the Tories to Black Mingo. Learning this from the swift mounted scouts whom he always kept a close hanging upon their march, Marion ordered us to face about, "dog" them to their encampment, and attack with great fury. Our fire commenced on them at a short distance and with great effect; but outnumbering us at least two to one, they stood their ground and fought desperately. Losing their commander and being hard – pressed, they at length gave way and fled in the utmost precipitation, leaving upwards of two thirds of their number, killed and wounded, on the ground.

This third exploit of Marion rendered his name very dearly to the poor Whigs but utterly abominable to the enemy, particularly the Tories, who were so terrified at this last handling, that, on their retreat, they would not halt a moment at Georgetown, though twenty miles from the field of battle; but they continued their flight, not thinking themselves safe until they had got Santee River between he and them.

Because of these three spirited charges, having cost us a great deal of rapid marching and fatigue, Marion said he would give us "a little rest." He led us down into Waccamaw where he knew we had some excellent friends, among whom were the Hugers, Trapiers, and Alstons—fine fellows! Such as Jews and hearty as we could wish; indeed, the wealthy captain, now Colonel William Alston, was one of Marion's aides. These great people received us as though we had been their brothers. They threw open the gates of their elegant yards for our cavalry, hurried us up their princely steps, and not withstanding our dirt and rags, ushered us into their grand salons and dining rooms, where the famous mahogany sideboards were quickly covered with pitchers of old amber colored brandy and sugar dishes of double refined, with honey, for drams and juleps. Our horses were up to their eyes in corn and sweet scented fodder, while as for ourselves, nothing that air, land, or water could furnish, was good enough for us. Fish, flesh, and fowl, all of the fattest and finest, and sweetly graced with the smiles of the great ladies, were spread before us, as though we had been kings for the British.

This was feasting indeed! It was a feasting of the soul, as well as of the senses. To have drawn the sword for liberty and dear country's sake, was, of itself, no mean reward to be honest Republicans; but beside that, to be so honored and caressed by the great ones of the land, was like throwing the zone of Venus over the waist of Minerva, or like crowning profit with pleasure, and duty with delight.

In consequence of the three fortunate blows which he had lately struck, Marion, as before observed, was getting the enviable honor of being looked upon as the rallying point of the poor Whigs. They were as afraid as mice to stir themselves, yet, if they found out that the Tories and the British were anywhere forming encampments about the country, they would spot them.

We had just gotten ourselves well braced up again, by rest and high feeding, among the noble Whigs of Waccamaw, when a likely young fellow at halspeed drove up one morning to the house and asked for General Marion.

Marion went to the door.

"Well, my son, what do you want with me?"

"Why, Sir General," replied the youth, "Daddy sent me down to let you know, as how there is to be a mighty gathering of the Tories in our parts tomorrow night."

"Aye indeed! And pray whereabouts, my son, may your parts be?"

"Heigh, Sir General! Don't you know where our parts is? I thought everybody knowed where Daddy lives."

"No, my son, I don't, but I've a notion he lives somewhere on PeeDee, perhaps a good way up."

"Yes, by jing, does he live a good way up! A matter of seventy miles, clean away up there, up on Little Pee Dee."

"Very well, my son. I thank your daddy and you, too, for letting me know it. And, I believe, I must try to meet the Tories there."

"O la, sir general, try to meet them indeed! Yes, to be sure! Dear me, sirs, hearts alive, that you must, Sir General! For Daddy says, as how, he is quite sartin, if you'll be there tomorrow night, you may make a proper smash among the Tories; for they'll be there thick and threefold. They have heard, so they say, of your doings, and you are going to hold this great meeting on purpose to come all the way down here after you."

"After me?"

"Yes, indeed are they, sir general! And you had better keep a sharp look out, I tell you now; for they have just been down to the British, there at Georgetown, and brought up a matter of two wagon loads of guns; great big English muskets! I can turn my thumb in them easy enough! And, besides them plaguy guns, they have got a tarnal nation sight of pistols! And bayonets! And swords! And saddles! And bridles! And the dear knows what else besides! So they are in a mighty good fix you may depend, Sir General."

"Well perhaps you and I may have some of them fine things tomorrow night. What say you to it, my son?"

"By jing, I should like it proper well! But, to be sure, now, Sir General, you look like a mighty small man to them great big Tories there, on Pee Dee. But Daddy says as how the heart is all; and he says, too, that though you are but a little man, you have a monsterous great heart."

Marion smiled and went out among his men, to whom he related the boy's errand; and he desired them to question him so that there might be no trick in the matter. Every scruple of that sort was quickly removed, for several of our party were well acquainted with the lad's father and knew him to be an excellent Whig.

Having put our firearms in prime order for an attack, we mounted, and giving our friend three cheers, we dashed off, just as the moon arose. By daybreak the next morning, we had gained a very convenient swamp within ten miles of the grand Tory rendezvous. To avoid giving alarm, we struck into the swamp, and there, man and horse, lay snug all day. At about eleven o'clock, Marion sent out a couple of nimble footed young men to conceal themselves near the main road and to take good heed to what was going on. In the evening, they returned and brought word that the road had been constantly alive with horsemen: Tories, they supposed, armed with new guns and all moving on very gaily towards the place the lad had told us of. As soon as it was dark, we mounted and took the track at a sweeping gallop, which by early supper time, brought us in sight of their fires. Then leaving their horses under a small guard, we advanced quite near them in the dark without being discovered. For so little thought had they of Marion that they had not placed a single sentinel but were all hands gathered about the fire: some cooking, some fiddling and dancing, and some playing cards, as we could hear them bawling every now and then.

Poor wretches! Little did they think how near the fates were grinning around them.

Observing that they had three large fires, Marion divided our little party of sixty men into three companies, each opposite to a fire. Then, bidding us to take aim, with his pistol, he gave the signal for a general discharge. In a moment, the woods were all in a blaze. Down tumbled the dead; off bolted the living; loud screamed the wounded; while far and wide, all over the woods, nothing was to be heard but the running of Tories and the snorting of wild bounding horses, snapping the saplings. Such a tragic comedy was hardly ever seen. On running up their fires, we found we had killed twenty – three and badly wounded as many more; thirteen we made prisoners; poor fellows who had not been grazed by a bullet, but were so frightened that they could not budge a peg. We got eighty four stand of arms, chiefly English muskets and bayonets, one hundred horses with new saddles and bridles, all English, too, with a good deal of ammunition and baggage. The consternation of the Tories was so great that they never dreamt of carrying off anything. Even their fiddles and fiddle bows and playing cards were all left strewed around their fires. One of the gamblers (it is a serious truth), though shot dead, still held the cards hard, gripped in his hands. Led by curiosity which he held were ace, deuce, and jack clubs trumps. Holding high, low, jack, and the game, in his own hand, he seemed to be in a fair way to do well; but Marion came down upon him with a trump that spoiled his sport and unsuited him forever.

The most comfortable sight of all was the fine supper which the Tories had cooked! Three fat roasted pigs and six turkeys with piles of journey cakes. 'This true, the dead bodies lay very thick round the fires, but having rode seventy miles and eating nothing since the night before, we were too keen set to think of standing on trifles; so, it fell upon the poor Tories's provisions, and it made the heartiest supper in the world. And to crown it all, we found among the spoil, upwards of half a barrel of fine old peach brandy.

"Ah, this brandy" said Marion, "was the worst foe these poor rogues ever had. But I'll take care it shall be no foe to us." So, after ordering half a pint to each man, he had the balance put under guard. And I must observe, by way of justice to my honored friend, that success never seemed to elate him; nor did ever he lose sight of safety in the blaze of victory. For instantly after the defeat, our guns were loaded and our sentinels set, as if an enemy had been in force in the neighborhood.

August 18, 1780

To Lieutenant Colonel Cruger, commander at the British garrison at Ninety-Six

Sir,

I have given orders that all inhabitants of this province, who had submitted, and who have taken part in this revolt, shall be punished with the greatest rigor, that they shall be imprisoned, and their whole property taken from them or destroyed. I have likewise directed that compensation should be made out of their effects, to persons who have been plundered and oppressed by them. I have ordered, in the most positive manner, that every militia man who had borne arms with us, and had afterwards joined the enemy, should be immediately hanged. I have now, Sir, only to desire that you will take the most vigorous measures to extinguish the rebellion in the district which you command, and that you will obey, in the strictest manner, the directions I have given in this letter, relative to the treatment of this country.

War-Torn South

This order of Lord Cornwallis proved to South Carolina like the opening of Pandora's box. Instantly, there broke forth a torrent of cruelties and crimes never before heard of in our simple forests. Lord Rawdon acted, as we shall see a shameful part in these bloody tragedies, and so did Colonel Tarleton. But the officer who figured most in executing the detestable orders of Cornwallis was a Major Weymies. This man, by birth, was a Scotsman; but in principle and practice, a Mohawk. So totally destitute was he of that amiable sympathy which belongs to his nation, that in sailing up Winyah Bay and the Waccamaw and Pee Dee rivers, he landed and pillaged and burnt every house he durst approach! Such was the style of his entry upon our afflicted state, and such the spirit of his doings throughout: for wherever he went, an unsparing destruction awaited upon his footsteps.

The dogs of hell were all now completely uncoupled, and every divine passion in man had its proper game.

A thievish Tory, who had been publicly whipped by a Whig magistrate or had long coveted his silver tankard, or his handsome rifle, or his elegant horse had but to point out to Major Weymies, and say, "there lives a damned rebel." The amiable major would surround the noble building in a trice; and after gutting it of all its furniture, would reduce it to ashes. It was in vain that the poor mother and children, on bended knees, with wringing hands and tear – swimming eyes implored him to pity, and not to burn their house over their heads. Such eloquence, which has often moved the breasts of savages was all lost on Major Weymies and his banditti. They no more regarded the sacred cries of children than the Indians do the cries of the young beavers, whose house they are breaking up.

A planter, in his fields, accidently turning towards his house, suddenly discovers a vast column of smoke bursting forth and ascending in black curling volumes to heaven. "Oh my God! My house!" he exclaims, "my poor wife and children." Then, half bereft of his senses, he sets and runs toward his house. Still, as he cuts the air, he groans out, "Oh, my poor wife and children." Presently, he hears their cries. He sees them in a distance with outstretched arms flying toward him. "Oh, Pa! Pa! Pa!" his children tremblingly exclaim. While his wife, all pale and out of breath, falls on his bosom and feebly cries out, "The British! Oh, the British!" and sinks into a swoon.

Who can tell the feelings of a father and the husband! His wife, his property all sinking to ruin by merciless enemies! Presently, his wife, after a strong fit, with a deep sigh, comes to herself. He wipes her tears, and he embraces and hushes the children. By and by, supposing the British to be gone, arm in arm, the mournful group return. But ah, the shocking sight of their once stately mansion which shone so beauteous on the plain, the pride and pleasure of their eyes is not the prey of a devouring flame. Their slaves have all disappeared. Their stock, part of it taken away, lies bleeding in the yard, stabbed by bayonets; their elegant furniture, tables, clocks, and beds are all swallowed up. An army of passing demons could have done no worse. But while with tearful eye, they are looking round the widespread ruin, undermined by the fire, down comes the tall building with a thundering crash to the ground. The frightened mourners stare aghast from the hideous squelch, and weep afresh to see all the hopes and glories of their state thus suddenly ended in smoke and ashes.

It was in this way exactly that the British treated my brother, Major Hugh Horry, as brave a soldier as ever fought in America. They laid in ashes all his dwelling houses, his barns of clean rice, and even his rice stalks. They destroyed his cattle and carried off eighty Negroes, which was all he had, not leaving him one to bake him a cake. Thus in one hour did the British serve my poor brother, breaking him up root and branch and, from a state of affluence, reducing him to a dunghill.

These savage examples, first set by the British and followed by the Tories, soon produced the effect that Marion had all along predicted. They filled the hearts of the sufferers with the deadliest hate of the British and brought them in crowds to join his standard with muskets in their hands and vows of revenge eternal in their mouths.

This was truly the case; for, every day, the Whigs were coming into Marion's camp. Those that were too old to fight themselves would call upon their sturdy boys to "turn out and join General Marion."

"Now Britons, look to your ships, for Carolina soon will be too hot to hold you."

The Swamp Fox continued to harass the enemy from his well-hidden camp on Snow's Island in the Pee Dee swamps. In December, he sent a scouting band out to explore the Black River ferry road. This band ran into a group of Tories under Major Ganey, who eventually ran wounded back to town. Marion and his men came in and leveled the fortifications. During the months of fighting which brought Francis Marion his fame, Georgetown had been his focal point: to recapture her from the enemy, his goal. With the enemy removed from the state except a twenty mile area of Charleston, voting for the assembling of the legislature, was held at Jacksonboro. Voting was held on December 17 and 18, 1781, at Shepard's Tavern on Black Mingo Creek for the Parish of Prince Frederick. Georgetown was used as the port of entry with the north while the British were still in Charleston. Stores of great proportion were kept for the army, and goods for future use were sent upriver to be stored in the neighborhood of Black Mingo Creek and along Black River, as well. In July 1782, the British again attacked Georgetown. The stores in town were sent hurriedly up the Black River. The Battle of Black Mingo resulted in the abandonment of the British plans for building a chain of forts through Williamsburg and was a turning point of the Revolutionary War in the South.

Heroes can be hard to find, but few were as intentional about it as Francis Marion, the Revolutionary War commander for whom about half the stuff around these parts are named. For the better part of two critical years in the struggle for American independence, Marion and his ragtag band bedeviled British and Loyalist forces in the South Carolina low country with their hit and run, guerilla warfare style tactics. Marion never had enough men to be tactically decisive, but by keeping the cause alive, and the Tories on edge, he played a surprisingly large role in the American victory. Marion's wartime work involved a lot of hiding out in the swamps of the Pee Dee and the marshes further east and south. That was great for eluding Redcoats, but not so good, it turns out, for living on in posterity. Late in September 1780, Marion left Snow's Island and proceeded up Lynch's Creek for the purpose of driving out the British and the Tories. General Marion camped near where the town of Cades now stands. His camping there gave the name Camp Branch to that vicinity for a hundred years. From that point, Marion proceeded on his way to Tarcote, crossing the lower ford on the North Branch of Black River at Nelson's Plantation and came upon the camp of Tyrnes at midnight. Tyrnes and his Tories were enjoying themselves. Some of them were sleeping, while others were eating and drinking or playing cards, but none of them were looking for the "Swamp Fox." Marion fell upon them immediately, killing twenty six and capturing Tyrnes and two of his officers and many of his men, without resistance on their part. Most of the Tories escaped through the swamp and never reassembled. General Marion secured many valuable supplies and was enabled from them to outfit his entire brigade. A little later, Tarleton, with a very superior force, attempted to capture Marion, while on the south branch of Black River. The story goes that Tarleton followed up Marion for many miles until the Britisher reached Ox Swamp. Looking over the way that Marion had gone (this miry waste), he exclaimed to his legion, "Come my boys, let us go back.

Another invasion of Williamsburg was attempted in 1781 when Lord Rawdon undertook to crush Marion in his rendezvous on Snows Island. Marion was advised by his scouts of these approaching British army almost as soon as they had left Fort Watson.

John Postell had been reared on a plantation above Georgetown. He knew every creek, path, and roadway along the lower Pee Dee. He was acquainted with every Whig and Tory in the district. As he inquired about salt, he learned from friends of an unguarded treasure on Waccamaw Neck. He reported his discovery to Marion: "Have heard of 150 bushels of salt on Waccamaw which the enemy intend to make use of to salt sixty head of cattle they have collected." Marion laconically informed Greene: "I have sent a party to bring it off."

What a precious commodity was salt! The manufacturers in All Saints Parish on Waccamaw Neck extracted it from sea water in huge evaporation vats and sold it for ten silver dollars a bushel. As few Whigs or Tories had gold or silver, their families ate unsalted meat and unsavory bread. With the instincts of a guerilla chief, who somehow provides necessities for his people even when he denies his troops, Marion sent a detachment with wagons and Sumpter's horses to bring off those 150 bushels. "As soon as Gen. Marion could collect a sufficient quantity of this desirable article at Snow's Island," James afterward wrote, "he distributed it out in quantities, not exceeding a bushel for each Whig family; and thus endeared himself the more to his followers."

December 29, 1780: That evening, Marion called in Captain John Postell and handed him a set of orders:

Snow's Island, December 30, 1780

Sir:

You will proceed with a party down Black River, from Black Mingo to the mouth of Pee Dee, and come up to this place; you will take all the boats and canoes from Euhaney up, and impress Negroes to bring them to camp; put some men to see them safe; you will take every horse, to whomsoever he may belong, whether friend or foe. You will take all arms and ammunition for the use of our service. You will forbid all persons from carrying any grains, stock, or any sort of provisions to Georgetown, or where the enemy may get them, on pain of being held as traitors and enemies to the Americans. All persons who will not join you will take prisoners and bring to me. You will return as soon as possible. Let me know any intelligence you may gain of the enemy's strength or movements.

I am, your obedient servant,
Francis Marion.
Adjt. Postell

N.B. – You will bring up as much rice and salt in the boats as possible.

Marion's force was not sufficiently strong to resist Watson, so he withdrew, marching down the river. Marion contested Watson's advance again at Mount Hope in Williamsburg. He burned the bridges that crossed Mount Hope Swamp; and while Watson's engineers were rebuilding them, his sharpshooters killed and wounded many. Watson's artillery could not fire effectively upon the ford without placing their guns in a position exposed to the deadly fire of McCottry's riflemen. Every attempt made to bring the field pieces to bear upon the low ground occupied by Marion's men resulted fatally for the artillerists. Watson attempted to rush the ford. The officers leading this forlorn hope fell from Captain McCottry's rifle. Captain McCottry's first shot was a signal for his riflemen along the banks to fire; and, as fast as the British approached, they fell before the unerring aim of McCottry's men. Watson was terrified of the fierce resistance that he had received. He said that he had never before seen such a shooting in all of his life. By that time, Marion was hurrying towards Snow's Island, having driven Watson out of Williamsburg. He arrived too late to meet Doyle; however, his brigade fired upon Doyle's forces as they were crossing Witherspoon's Ferry on their way back to Camden.

After retiring to Snow's Island, at the confluence of Lynches Creek and the Pee Dee River, Francis Marion fortified himself in a more permanent camp than before. The date of his encampment was the first of the year in 1781 and abounded with livestock and provisions. Francis Marion first secured all the boats in the vicinity and after reserving a few for his need, destroyed all the rest. The bridges were all broken up and destroyed, for his men needed no bridges to cross the river. He obstructed the banks of the river at crossing places by falling trees. Parties were sent out to scour the countryside and report any movement. It was at the encampment on the island that the famous potatoes dinner took place. The story is that a British officer arrived at Marion's encampment with a flag of truce to negotiate an exchange of prisoners. After being blindfolded and escorted to the camp, and his business finished, he was about to depart. Francis Marion then invited him to stay and share his dinner. The British officer looked around: an open fire, but no food anywhere. Out of curiosity, or politeness, or both, he accepted the invitation. Francis Marion then directed his faithful servant, Oscar, to serve dinner. When the servant came forth bearing dinner, it was no more than sweet potatoes, roasting on an open fire, dug out of the glowing ashes and served on pieces of clean pine bark! General Marion ate heartily and urged his guests to do the same. The officer ate the potatoes out of politeness, but his politeness could not prevent him from inquiring if this food was the usual fare. Francis Marion told the officer that they were fortunate that day in there were more potatoes than usual. The British officer looked at the men who passed before them and decided their pay was no better than their food. The officer returned to the garrison at Georgetown much impressed by what he has heard and seen that day. He was so convinced of the impossibility of overcoming soldiers who lived on so little and fought for the pure love of liberty, that he resigned his commission. He returned to England thinking that who fought so valiantly for freedom deserved it. It was very important that people had the bridge built in order for the Swamp Fox to be so very successful.

It is true that Marion's men were sometimes poorly supplied with clothing and with provisions and that often they dressed in the skins of animals they had slain and lived on sweet potatoes and fish, and fought with the swords their women had filed out of handsaws and shot the bullets these same women had molded from their pewter spoons. Cornwallis said after the war, on being taunted on account of his inability to destroy Marion in Williamsburg, "I could not capture web footed men who could subsist on roots and berries." He was thinking of the ability of Marion's men to cross the swamps in Williamsburg and of their potato diet.

The four Nesmith brothers—John, Robert, Samuel, and Lemuel—were General Marion's bodyguards. These Nesmiths were herdsmen in their boyhood days and knew the country from following the cattle. They were exceptionally physical men, each one of them more than six feet tall. They were as active and alert as Indians, and everyone was an expert riflemen. They all loved their leader with surpassing loyalty and devotion. Tradition says that General Marion and a Continental officer with a message from General Green to General Marion were discussing conditions at Tarcote when a body of Tories under Major Gillis appeared in the distance. General Marion and the Continental officer stood their ground, but the four Nesmith brothers disappeared immediately behind a little milk house. Marion understood, but the Continental officer doubted their actions. The Tories came on. When their leader had arrived at a point about three hundred yards from General Marion, four rifles from behind the milk house shot as one, and the Tory leader fell. His followers fled. General Marion and the Continental officer walked up to the body of the dead Tory. General Marion placed his hands over the heart of the dead man and asked the Continental officer to locate the wound. The four Nesmith brothers had each placed a bullet in the space covered by Marion's hand. The Continental officer then told General Marion that he would go back to General Green and tell him that the swamps of South Carolina were safe for liberty.

The American Revolutionary War, On October 7, 1780, the battle of Kings Mountain was fought, sparking the series of event that eventually led to England's loss of America. The situation for the rebellious colonies looked bleak in 1778. In an attempt to end the war, the British had turned their efforts to the South, launching a full-scale invasion in the autumn of 1778.

By 1780, the British controlled Georgia and had won important victories at Charleston and Camden. Lord Cornwallis, British commander in the South, believed that South Carolina was won.

Turning his attention to North Carolina, he began to march from Charleston. Cornwallis hoped to invade North Carolina at Charlotte by September. One of his officers, Maj. Patrick Ferguson was to move through the up country of the South Carolina border, wiping out patriot resistance and protecting the flank and rear of Cornwallis' advancing army. After moving across the western North Carolina border, Ferguson established his base at Gilbert Town, today the site of Rutherfordton. Ferguson underestimated the local people and their desire to take up arms against the British. He threatened to "hangs their leaders and to lay their country to waste with fire and sword." Rather than cowering, the citizens stiffened their opposition. A call went out to mobilize against the hated British.

On September 25:

At Sycamore Shoals near the present town of Elizabethton, Tennessee, more than a thousand volunteers assembled. The next day the famous march over the mountains began. Meanwhile, Ferguson had been warned of the formidable force that was being organized against him. Unknown to the patriots Ferguson left Gilbert Town heading toward Ninety Six. He also sent an urgent message to Cornwallis asking for reinforcements. Unfortunately for Ferguson, his message did not reach Cornwallis until after the battle. Instead of marching to Ninety-Six, Ferguson hastened toward Charlotte, North Carolina. hoping that the patriots would not learn of his diversionary move.

The American patriot force reached Gilbert Town on October 4. Learning that Ferguson and his troops were no longer there, the patriots took after the British in hot pursuit. The patriots were fortunate volunteers, bringing the total to 1,800 fighting men. At Cowpens a select group to the toughest fighting in the patriotic forced was chosen to overtake Ferguson. After an exhausting overland march, the patriots arrived near Kings Mountain on Oct. 7.

The Battle of Kings Mountain lasted only about an hour and resulted in a complete victory for the patriots. The British relied on the bayonet. The patriots relied on their marksmanship and the deadly accuracy of their Kentucky rifles. After withstanding several bayonets by the British, the patriots surrounded and disorganized the enemy. Ferguson made one futile attempt to rally his troops but was shot dead by sharpshooters. The British surrendered. The patriots' surprising and devastating victory at Kings Mountain changed the course of the Revolutionary War. The immediate result was the delay of Cornwallis' northward march and the abandonment of his stronghold at Charlotte. The moral of the patriots was boosted, Resistance to the British increased, and the patriotic forces began to take the offensive.

In 1951, Congress, in recognition of the Nation significance of the site of battle, established the Kings Mountain National Military Park, creating a lasting monument to those valiant patriots who fought in the American Revolution.

Skirmish at Black Mingo Creek

September 14, 1780: General Marion's troops routed the Tories under Captain J Comming Ball. Attacked on one flank by Captain Thomas Waites and on the other by Col. Horry with General Marion's reserves in rear, the Tories fled into Black Mingo Swamp. The action was so sharply contested that each side lost nearly one third of its men. Killed and wounded, Captain Henry Mouzon and Lieutenant Joseph Scott were both wounded there and were carried to White Marsh in North Carolina, where they remained until their recovery.

At the age of twenty-seven, Marion began his military career as a volunteer in the first Cherokee war. His valor and natural skill as a soldier caused Gov. Rutledge to commission him lieutenant in the second Cherokee War. In 1775, when Marion again volunteered to serve under Moultrie in the defense of Charlestown against the British fleet, he was made captain in the second South Carolina Regiment. It was during the defense of Fort Johnson, (afterwards called fort Moultrie), on Sullivan's Island that the first flag of America was displayed. There being no official colors for American troops, Gen. Moultrie, for signaling purposes, designed a blue flag with a silver star and crescents in the dexter corner to match the blue uniforms of the First and Second South Carolina regiments, who wore a crescent on their caps. Thus, 'the bonnie blue flag' of South Carolina fluttered on the breezes over an American fort before the stars and stripes were designed for Gen. Washington by Betsy Ross. Gen. Moultrie's blue flag was later adopted by the state legislature with the addition of a palmetto in the center to commemorate the importance played in the defense of the fort by the spongy palmetto logs of which the fort was constructed and in which the enemy's cannonballs were harmlessly embedded. A beautiful blue silk banner with the silver star and crescent was embroidered by 'Col. Elliott's lady and presented the gallant South Carolina troops. Sergeant (William) Jasper's immortal heroism in defending these colors had made them doubly sacred to South Carolinas.

Old Fort Watson

The Scene of a Famous Exploit by General Marion by Mrs. Samuel J. Clark:

Nine miles southwest of the thriving town of Summerton, near the beautiful crescent-shaped Scott's Lake, stands old Fort Watson of revolutionary fame. This pile of earth about thirty-five feet in height, and 150 feet in circumference was, at one time, an Indian mound rising abruptly from a level field. Upon beholding it for the first time, one naturally wonders where the material of which it is made came from. Its perpendicular sides are covered with vines and shrubbery, and upon its summit are venerable oaks, draped in gray Spanish moss. Near its base lap the yellow waters of the lake, and over all broods an indescribable calm and peace.

Oh, brother pilgrim on life's journey, have you grown weary of the burden and the heat of the day? Would you fain call a moment's "cool halt" and rest for a while far from the dust and din of the world's machinery? If so, seek this historic spot where the grandeur and beauty of the scenery and the solitude combined cause the creature to feel nearer to his Creator.

During the first years of the revolutionary war, Fort Watson was occupied by the British, and situated directly on the road between Camden and Charleston. It was an important base of supplies for the British army. So anxious were the Americans to capture this fort that General Sumter, on one occasion, with a small force, swam the Santee and boldly attacked the enemy. His efforts were futile, however, and the Americans retreated with heavy losses.

In 1782, while Colonel Rawdon, who commanded the British forces, had his main army at Camden, a unique plan was made to capture Fort Watson. During one entire night, the forest bordering the Santee River rang with the sound of the woodmen's axe and when the rising sun gilded the yellow waters of the lake and river, its rays shown upon tower of logs that overlook the fort. From this tower, a deadly fire rained down upon the British, who, taken by surprise, were routed. Down came the haughty ensign that had long waved there, and from the wooded crest of old Fort Watson floated the Stars and Stripes.

In the early seventies, the country of the vicinity of the old fort was not isolated as it is today; a short distance from it was Wright's Bluff, at the time a shipping point of considerable importance. In fact, at one time, figuratively speaking, "all roads in Clarendon led to Wright's Bluff." The steamboats *Marion*, *Louisa*, *Planter*, and *Santee*, with their jovial and polite captains, were met by crowds from every section of the country. The railroads had changed all things with its stern iron will, and Wright's bluff is totally abandoned. At that time, Fort Watson, commonly called "the Mound," bore the reputation of being haunted; many persons claimed to have seen a very white object near its base and belated travelers usually gave the place a wide berth.

One night, a gentleman, who lived about two miles from Wright's Bluff and who had been detained there rather later than usual, was riding home quite leisurely. Absorbed in his own reflections, he scarcely knew where he was going when suddenly his gentle horse snorted and leaped, almost unseating his rider. Greatly surprised, he tried to quiet his horse. Glancing about him he saw that he was very near Fort Watson. Just then the moon that had been obscured by scudding clouds shone upon a ghostly white object standing near the mound. This gentleman had been a fearless Confederate soldier and had often stood unflinchingly amid a storm of shot and shell, yet when telling me this story, he confessed that he caught himself on that night pressing his hat down upon his head as his hair rose in horror beneath it.

As his horse refused to approach this object, he dismounted and, after fastening him securely to a small tree, set out alone to meet the apparition. When he stood within a few feet of it, he beheld a meek-looking white cow, and lo, the mystery of the mound was solved.

Standing on the magnificent trees and bold bluffs skirting the lake, he feels that he is in some land enchanted and finds it hard to realize that this place was once the scene of strife.

The State

October 27, 1912

All letters are as written:

Snow's Island 14th January 1781

[This letter published as written in old English by the Swamp Fox]

Yours of the seventh day, I have received the ammunition care to hand. In my last I acquainted you that Col. Campbell commanded in Geo town. But what Corps? I cannot learn. I sent a detachment of fifty men under Col. Peter Horry on Waccamaw Neck to collect the boats & drive off the cattle, near Capt. Allston's he met with the British about 20 horse round. His advance party to his main body which gave them a fire repulsed and pursued them to their main body consisting of sixty men under Col. Campbell which obliged Col. Horry to retreat. The emery had three men & four horses killed, and took two prisoners which proved to the Queens rangers. We had one man slightly wounded and two horses killed. I have sent reinforcement to Col. Horry who informed me the emery had one galley & an armed vessel come up tumbrels Plant. Eight miles higher up the river than when he met the emery the day before & by his information they had landed fifty infantry & a body of horse said to be fifty joined them from below. But I believe it to be the same party as I do not think they could spare so many from Georgetown, & I not learnt they have had any late reinforcement, my opinion is that they mean to come up to Bull's Creek & have the command of Waccamaw & PeeDee rivers down to Georgetown to co – operate with a body of Tory which lay at Amey's Plant on Drowned Creek near the line of North Carolina. This body of Tories consists by report of 150 men commanded by one Hector McNeil. I think this body of men is dangerous as they will collect a large number of Tories from N. Carolina the enemy possessing themselves of Waccamaw Neck will give them a large extent of country which contains a great quantity of provisions of all kinds. I should have marched my whole body against those Tories but I should be oblige to withdraw all my detachments which would leave fifty miles open to the enemy, sand inhabitants finding their property & families exposed will desert me almost to a man – Last week I had ordered Col. Kolbs regiment to march to Little Pee Dee & sent Major Vandercrst with a detachment to meet him & to disperse the Torys under McNeil but Col. Kolb never obeyed this order & the major after going up as far as Maiden town high up the cat – fish was oblige to return – I have again ordered Col. Kolb to join me with all his regiment if he comes in time I hope to remove the Torys & oblige the British on Waccamaw to retire to their garrison I am much afraid of the dilatorines of this officer. I think it absolutely is necessary they should be attacked without loss of time. If it cannot be done by a force from you I must draw in my detachments. As soon as I hear more particularly of the enemy from Col. Horry will acquaint you – I have the honor to be yr. Opt. Servt. Francis Marion

Colonel Marion to Colonel P. Horry:

Lynch's Creek, Aug 17, 1780

Sir,

You will take the command of such men as will be collected from Capts. Bounnesu's, Mitchell's and Benson's companies, and immediately proceed to Santee, from the lower ferry to Lenud's, and destroy all the boats and canoes on the river, and post guards at each crossing place, to prevent persons from crossing to or from Charleston, on either side of the river. You will give all necessary intelligence, and the number of men you may have collected as early as possible. You will procure about twenty-five weight of gun powder, and a proportionable quantity of ball or swan shot, also flints, and send them up to me immediately, to the Kingstree, by an express.

I am with esteem,
Your obedient servant,
FRANCIS MARION

N.B. You will also take the command of Capt. Lenud's Company, and the furnish your men with arms, wherever you can find them receipts.

Brigadier General Marion to Adjutant Postell:

Snow's Island, December 30, 1780

SIR,

You will proceed with a party down Black river, from Black Mingo to the Mouth of PeeDee, and come up to this place; you will take all the boats and canoes from Euhaney up, and impress negroes to bring them to camp; put some men to see them safe; you will take all arms and ammunition for the use of our service. You will forbid all persons from carrying any grains, stock or any sort of provisions to Georgetown, or where the enemy may get them, on pain of being held as traitors and enemies to the Americans. All persons who will not join you will take prisoners and bring to me. You will return as soon as possible. Let me know any intelligence you may gain of the enemy's strength or movements.

I am your obedient servant,

FRANCIS MARION.

Adjt. Postell.

N.B.--- You will bring up as much rice and salt in the boat as possible.

Gen. Marion to Capt. John Postell:

Goddard's Plantation, PeeDee, Jan. 19, 1781.

DEAR SIR,

I send Lieut. King with fifteen men, to reinforce you. I would have all the flats and boats you can collect, loaded with rice, and salt to Mr. Joseph Allston's plantation, on Bull's creek, to the "North of PeeDee, where there is a ferry to Euhaney; and the rice is to be there stored, and the boats kept going until all that is to beat out in your district is carried. From there I will send for it up higher. You must take such negroes for the boats as belong to those persons who may be with the enemy, or from those estates which the enemy think forfeited, Gen. Greene is in want of a number of negroes--, say fifty--- for the use of the army. You will collect them in your district, and send them to me; taking I shall detain those negroes that came up with the boats you have sent. One boat has arrived, and I have sent to assist in getting up the others. I beg you if possible, their particular strength: what corps of horse and foot, and how many militia, and if there are any cannon mounted on their redoubt, and whether they are making any new works. You will send Capt. W----, and Mr. S----, and all such men (who have taken, or are suspected of having taken part with the enemy) to me. You must not suffer any person to carry property where the enemy has possession, or have any intercourse with them.

I am, with regard, dear Sir,
Your obedient servant,
Francis Marion.

Extract of a Letter from General Marion to Captain Postell:

January 19, 1781.

DEAR SIR,

Your father may keep the canoe you mention. I have received the prisoners, by Mr. M'Pherson, and shall give them the pleasure of seeing head quarters.

I am, dear Sir,

Your obedient servant,

FRANCIS MARION.

Brigadier General Marion to Captain John Postell:

January 23, 1781

SIR,

Particular circumstances make me desire that you will immediately march all the men under your command to join me at Kingstree; you must proceed by forced marches until you come up to me for no time is to be lost. Leave your post as secretly as possible, without letting any one know where you are going, or of your intention to leave it.

I am, dear Sir,
Your obedient servant,
Francis Marion

General Marion to Captain John Postell:

Corde's Plantation, January 29, 1781

FRANCIS MARION

DEAR SIR,

You will cross Santee river with twenty-five men, and make a forced march to Watboo bridge, there burn all the British stores of every kind; it is possible you will find a small guard there, which you may surprise, but bring no prisoners with you. You will return the same way, and recross the river at the same place, which must be done before daylight next morning. After effecting my purpose at Watboo, it will not be out of your way to come by Monk's corner, and destroy any stores or waggons you may find there. You can learn from the people at Watboo what guard there is at the corner; if it should be too strong you will not attempt that place. In going to Watboo, you must see if there is a guard at the church; if there is you will shun; you will consider provisions of all kinds British property. The destruction of all the British stores in the above-mentioned places is of the greatest consequence to us, and only requires boldness and expedition. Take care that your men do not get at liquor, or clog themselves with plunder so as to endanger their retreat.

I am with regard, dear Sir,
Your obedient servant,
Francis Marion

General Marion to Lieutenant-Colonel Balour:

Santee, March7, 1781.

SIR,

I sent Capt. John Postell with a flag to exchange some prisoners, which Capt. Saunders, commandant of Georgetown, had agreed to, but contrary to the law of nations, he has seized and detained as a prisoner. As I cannot imagine that his conduct will be approved by you, I hope orders will be immediately given to have my flag discharged, or I must immediately acquaint congress of this violation. The ill consequence of which it is now in your power to prevent. I am sorry to complain of the ill treatment my officers and men meet with from Capt. Saunders; the officers are closely employed in a small place, where they can neither stand or lie at length, nor have they more than half rations. I have treated your officers and men who have fallen into my hands in a different manner. Should these evils not be prevented in future, it will not be in my power to prevent retaliation. Lord Rawdon and Col. Watson have hanged three men of my brigade for supposed crimes, which will make as many of your men in my hands suffer. I hope this will be prevented in future, for it is my wish men in my hands to act with humanity and tenderness to those unfortunate men, the chances of war may throw in my power.

I have the honour to be
Your obedient servant,
Francis Marion

General Marion to Colonel Watson of the British:

Santee, March 7, 1781

SIR,

Enclosed is a letter which I wish may be forwarded as soon as possible. I make no doubt but that you will be surprised to see a flag sent at the head of an armed party. The reason of it is, that Capt. Saunders, commandant of Georgetown, has violated the law of nations, by taking, detaining and imprisoning Capt. Postell, who carried prisoners to exchange, which was agreed to by him. The hanging of prisoners and violation of my flag will be retaliated if a stop is not put to such proceedings, which are disgraceful to all civilized nation. All of your officers and men who have fallen into my hands, have been treated with humanity and tenderness; and I wish sincerely that I may not be obliged to act to my inclinations; but such treatment as my unhappy followers, whom the chances of war may throw in the hands of my enemies receive, such may those expect who fall in my hands.

I have the honour to be
Your obedient servant,
Francis Marion

General Marion to General Greene

Fort Watson, (Scott's Lake) April 23, 1781

SIR,

Lieut, Col. Lee made a junction with me at Santee, the ins. after a rapid march from Ramsay's mill, on Deep river, which he performed in eight days, The 15th we marched to this place and invested it. Our hope was to cut off their water. Some riflemen and continentals immediately took post between the fort and the lake. The fort is situated on a small hill, forty feet high, stockaded, and with three rows of abates around it. No trees near enough to cover our men from their fire. The third day after we had invested it, we found the enemy had sunk a well near the stockade, which we could not prevent them from; as we had no entrenching tools to make our approach, we immediately determined to erect a work equal in height to the fort. This arduous work was completed this morning by Major Maham, who undertook it. We then made a lodgment on the side of the mount near the stockade. This was performed with great spirit and address by Ensign Johnson and Mr. Lee, a volunteer in Col. Lee's legion, who with difficulty ascended the hill and pulled away the abbatis, which induced the commandant to hoist a flag; and Col. Lee and myself agreed to the enclosed capitulation, which I hope may be approved of by you. Our loss on this occasion is two killed, and three continentals and three militia wounded. I am particularly indebted to Col. Lee for his advice and indefatigable diligence in every part of these tedious operations, against as strong a little post as could be well made, and on the most advantageous spot that could be wished for. The officers and men of the legion and militia, performed everything that could be expected, and Major Maham, of my brigaded, had, in erecting a tower which principally occasioned the reduction of the fort. In short, Sir, I had the greatest assistance from every one under my command. Enclosed is a list of the prisoners and stores taken, and I shall, without loss of time, proceed to demolish the fort; after which I shall march to the High Hills of Santee, encamp at Capt. Richardson's, and await your orders.

(signed) FRANCIS MARION.

He was forever in the swamps in a series of base camps, the best known of which is Snow's Island, and he was most certainly the fox. Very cautious, very suspicious, knowing that the partisan must live to fight another day, he was never rash in the attack and was never reluctant to retreat. The hit, the run, and the ambush were his stock in trade.

The nature of the warfare in which he engaged was especially vicious, for the fighting in South Carolina was more akin to a civil conflict, and the grand rules of generals did not apply. Personal vendettas, house burning, looting, murder, and mayhem were the order of the day, and when not under his direct command, Marion's men were as brutal as any. While his methods were unorthodox, he never suffered such abuses in his presence. He was, Peter Horry said, "very human and merciful," and he insisted on as much discipline as the times allowed. There were no duels fought by men under his personal command.

He seems to have kept the fight alive largely through willful determination, and there were occasions when the strain sent him into brooding despair, and he thought of fleeing the state and even of resigning his commission. Feeling ignored, unaided, and unappreciated, he could grow testy over matters of rank and command. He never got along with Thomas Sumter and frequently had difficulties with Nathaniel Greene. Surprisingly, he worked fairly well with the flamboyant Lighthorse Harry Lee. Through all of this, Marion stayed in the field, and the fighting continued well after the surrender of Cornwallis at Wadboo Creek in the summer of 1782.

General Horatio Gates finally came, heading a large army, and planning to stomp the British. He was considered brilliant after his great victory for the Americana at Saratoga, but he was also arrogant and reckless. He rushed to meet the British at Camden, and in his haste, made several mistakes, which lead to a crushing defeat on

August 16, with the remnants of his fastest retreats in military history back across North Carolina.

Francis Marion had met briefly with Gates, who did not think much of Marion and his handful of rag tag militia. More to get them out of the way than anything, he sent them to scout the British and to try to destroy any boats or bridges that they might use on their expected retreat. Marion followed his orders well, returning down the upper Santee, burning boats, and destroying anything that would be of advantage to the British. As he did, he followed, for the rest of the war, a policy that did much to win over a lot of fence-sitters. He instructed his men to give receipts to the owner of any property that was confiscated or destroyed.

Many of these receipts were redeemed for payment after the war, and they are valuable records of the war's progress. Marion became a hero to the people, while the British Colonel Tarleton was hated. Tarleton became known as "Bloody Tarleton." Not only had he been the cause of the "Waxhaw Massacre," but he had gone on a campaign of pillaging the countryside, burning homes and crops, slaughter cattle, and taking anything of value. As he and his twenty militia men tried to get a little sleep, he heard the first shots of the Battle of Camden. Leaving off from his river duties, he hurried to Witherspoon Ferry (now Johnsonville), where he had been assigned to meet and command the Williamsburg Militia.

As Marion took command on August 17, he had not yet received news of the terrible loss of Gates army at Camden. The next morning he sent Colonel Peter Horry to the lower Santee to continue destroying ferryboats and to garner what supplies he could. He was in desperate need of powder and shot. Then Marion and some of his new command returned to the upper Santee to continue to prevent the British escape by cutting off any possible ferries. While there he received the news of Gate's loss at Camden, and had the awful realization that the Continental Army was not going to save South Carolina from the British.

Still, he was able to win a small victory right away. He did not tell his own troops right away of the American loss at Camden. From a Tory deserter he got word that thirty-eight British soldiers were camped overnight with American prisoners from Gate's arm, on the way back to Charleston at Nelson's Ferry (on the Wateree River west of Sumter). In a surprise dawn attack he killed and captured twenty-two of the escorting British troops and released the prisoners who had been part of Maryland line. To his surprise and chagrin, they would not join with his militia. They thought all was lost and the war would soon be over. Once freed, all but three of them deserted. (Sixty of them eventually made it back to their corps on the American side, but the rest just disappeared.) By August 26, Marion and his men were back at Witherspoon Ferry. He sent instructions to Colonel Horry to leave off from his assignment at the Santee and meet him quickly at Britain's Neck.

While Marion was capturing the prisoners, the only other force in South Carolina that was comparable to Marion's Brigade—Thomas Sumter's militia—lost badly at Fishing Creek, and Sumter barely escaped with his life. Sumter had become lax and did not have sufficient knowledge of the enemy. "Bloody" Tarleton surprised his unit while they were relaxed and resting. In a quick attack the British got between the men and their stacked muskets, so they could not fight. Sumter fled on horseback, getting away only because he had a pistol and was able to shoot the horse from under a pursuer.

Marion did not despair at the low ebb of the American tide in South Carolina. He knew he had to move quickly or the morale of the American patriots would be destroyed. He began a policy of hitting the British and their Tory allies, then quickly fading back into the woods, before they could organize counterattacks. Sometimes during the next few months, the Williamsburg militia became Marion's Brigade and Col. Marion became a general. The record of his commissioning has been lost.

Marion was more of a professional soldier than the men he led. He had fought in the earlier Indian War, and he had fought with the regulars at Charleston. When he took command of the Williamsburg militia (which included far more than Williamsburg County of today) he had a unit of citizen soldiers-men without a lot of military training, but men who were fighting for their own homes on their own turf. They were always short of supplies and had to live off the land and the people whom they were defending.

For arms, Marion's men mainly had the Brown Bess, an iron-barreled musket that fired a .75 caliber ball. Muskets took a while to reload, so army formation typically deployed musket-men in two or three lines. The first line would fire in unison, then drop to their knees to reload, while the lines behind them fired.

Because muskets were not accurate, musket-men were not even expected to aim at particular targets. Rather, the objective was to deliver a mass of musket-balls into the enemy line. The British troops were drilled and drilled until they could coolly, whether or not their orders made sense fire several volleys of disciplined musket fire, followed by a screaming bayonet charge. The British had seventeen-inch bayonets; the cold steel fire fear in their enemies, even when they had previously stood their ground against volleys of shot.

But Marion's style of fighting rarely gave the British a chance to use their cold steel. Marion used surprise to best advantage, because he had native scouts who knew the terrain. He would hit the British when they did not expect a battle, then fade into the woods before the British could even form battle lines. Sometimes the British troops never had a chance to fire a single shot.

A few highly treasured rifles came into Marion's Brigade. Unlike the smooth bored muskets, these accurately delivered a spinning bullet to hit a man's head at two hundred yards. They were still flintlocks, meaning that the gunpowder was ignited by a spark from metal striking flint. All of the guns used loose gunpowder made from salt-peter ("black-powder"); modern smokeless powder did not come until the latter part of the nineteenth century. Lead was treasured, and used sparingly to mold musket balls and rifle bullets as needed. Black powder was made from powdered charcoal and bat guano (dung) found in caves.

At the beginning, Marion's men mostly had their own guns, formerly used for hunting game. They did not have bayonets. So Marion commandeered the saw blades from some sawmills in this area, and had local black-smith make swords for his men, should they fall into hand to hand combat. Sawmills of that day did not have round (rotary) blades. Their blades were similar to the old two-man saws previously used for sawing boards by hand, one man, the top man, stood on the log, and the second, the pit man stood underneath in a hole or under a framework that held the log. When water power became available the back and forth motion was created by a spinning wheel with a knob near the outer edge, to which was attached an arm. This apparatus became called, understandable, a pitman. Common steel was not hard enough to hold a keen edge, unless it was tempered, then it would become brittle. So Marion had to find high quality steel. This was why he chose to use saw blades. Swords that were heated and hammered from these saw blades were then tempered for hardness. They could then be kept keen, but they did not break in use.

With these rude weapons, Marion began his campaign. They would have to do, until he could capture more modern (for that day) weapons that had been given to the Tories by the British. After seizing Charleston, the British moved inland and defeated the Continental forces at the Battle of Camden. The day before the action, Marion had been sent east to command the patriot militia between the Santee and the Pee Dee rivers. Again he had escaped defeat and capture. For months, Marion and his militiamen were the only opposition the British faced in South Carolina. Then, Marion began to fight back. From the fields, forests, and swampland of South Carolina's low country, Marion mustered the sons and grandsons of Huguenot, Scottish-Irish, and English immigrants. Many were sons of the Pee Dee: rugged, self-reliant men who had wrested small farms from the wilderness. They were comfortable on horseback, and they knew the region's swampy bogs and trails. They knew how to endure hardship and how to fight guerilla-style.

Each man was responsible for supplying his rations and his horse. They fashioned saw blades into swords and molded their musket balls from pewter plates. Their numbers ranged from 40 to 400, and they seldom had enough men to fight a conventional battle. Tarleton and his cavalry had butchered scores of disarmed Continental troops after they had surrendered. To catch Marion, Tarleton drove his men relentlessly, setting traps, dispatching patrols, and stumbling through mud, moss, and mosquitoes in futile pursuit. Instead, they struck with stealth, often attacking at night, and when pursued they would outdistance the enemy in the gloomy swamps. Then they would stop and stage an ambush, cutting up their pursuers in the crossfire.

Between raids, Marion and his men retreated to swampland hideaways like Snow's Island. The island became his most famous hideout, shielding Marion and his men like a fox's lair. Hidden there among the cypress and thickets, living off wild game and sweet potatoes, Marion planned his raids.

In 1780, the British launched a campaign to subdue South Carolina and conquer the new American states one by one until the rebellion was suppressed. But Marion's bold fighters attacked British outposts, disrupted supply lines and cut communications. Hampered by the lightening guerilla strikes, the British strategy stalled. To eliminate Marion and his men, the British high command dispatched Lieutenant Colonel Banastre Tarleton and his ruthless Green Dragoons. "Bloody Ban" Tarleton, as he was known in South Carolina, must have seemed the perfect choice to destroy Marion. Near Waxhaws, near Camden, Tarleton finally called a halt. His winded horseman had not even caught sight of Marion. "Come on my boys," he shouted, "let us go back. As for this damned old Fox, the Devil himself could not catch him." Tarleton never caught Marion, but he did give him his historic nickname—the Swamp Fox.

Finally in 1782, after the British strategy collapsed at Yorktown, Marion had the satisfaction of watching the British army sail away for the England. The Revolution had ended in victory for the Americans, and Francis Marion's grueling war with the British became history. After the war Marion finally married. He retained a command in the state militia and served in the state senate. His last years, however, were spent at his cherished plantation experimenting with methods of growing indigo. There, in the heart of the South Carolina Low Country he had fought so hard to protect, the old soldier died quietly on February 26, 1795, at the age of sixty-three.

A decade after Marion's death, an itinerant biographer named Mason Weems produced a book called The Life of General Francis Marion, which became a national best seller. Francis Marion became an American hero, whose name was bestowed in honor on new towns and counties from South Carolina to Iowa. Lakes, forests and colleges bore his name and a generation of American boys grew up christened as "Marion." In the Pee Dee, obscure Snow's Island retained a fame of its own as the fox's lair—hideaway of the great and glorious swamp Fox.

One of Francis Marion's escapades took place at Black Mingo Bridge. The Tories had been active in the area. The men in General Marion's Brigade had cares other than to their country. Their families were often threatened while they were away, and they had young ones at home who needed food and sometimes shelter. When the General found his men anxious about their families, his good judgment and kindness caused him to take their concerns into consideration. He yielded to their wishes, and this always had a good effect. They always returned at the time they agreed to. When word of the Tories laying waste to all the farms, plantations, schools, and churches reached Marion, he was short of men for giving them leave to go see about their families. The British were destroying family homes. He was away from Snow's Island at the time and was returning from the White Marsh in North Carolina. Traveling night and day, he hurried through the Tory settlements along Little Pee Dee. At Lynches Creek, he was met by Captains James and Mouzon.

The British soldier trembles when Marion's name is told. Marion's men equipped themselves by the capture from the enemy. They supported and sustained themselves from their plantations and were neither paid nor promised payment by any state authority. With these untrained pioneer backwoodsmen, Francis Marion took from the British the Pee Dee section of South Carolina, one third of the state (and while they were making frantic efforts to capture him). He held it against them for nearly a year before any American force succeeded in holding an acre of territory in the state for a single day after the fall of Charles Towne on May 12, 1772. The complete collapse of the state agencies—civil and military—Francis Marion was of the very few South Carolinians who actually separated from England. Almost every other man in the state was happy again to be safe within the arms of the "Mother Country." Marion's labors in the Pee Dee country saved South Carolina and Georgia for independence and the American union. His services from 1780 to 1783 make the most dramatic and colorful chapter in American history. The half of his story has never been told.

The Swamp Fox and his men would sit around a campfire and sing this song, composing as they went along. Remember this was the Revolutionary War, and the soldiers wrote in old English:

> Our brand is few but true and tried,
> Our leader frank and bold;
> The British soldier trembles,
> When Marion's name is told;
> Our fortress is the good greenwood,
> Our tent the cypress tree;
> We know the forest round us,
> As seamen know the sea.
> We know its wall of thorny vines,
> Its glades of reedy grass,
> It's safe and silent islands
> Within the dark morass.
>
> Woe to the English soldiery
> The little dread us near!
> On them shall shine at midnight
> A strange and sudden fear:
> When, waking to their tents on fire,
> They grasp their arms in vain,
> And they who stand to face us
> Are beat to earth again;
> And they who fly in terror deem
> A mighty host behind,
> And hear the tramp of thousands
> Upon the hollow wind.
>
> And sweet the hour that brings release
> From danger and from toil:
> We talk the battle over,
> And share the battle's spoil.

FRANCIS MARION

The woodland rings with laugh and shout,
As if a hunt was up,
And woodland flowers are gathered
To crown the soldier's cup.
With merry songs we mock the wind
That in the pine tops grieves,
And slumber long and sweetly
Our beds of oaken leaves

Well knows the fair and friendly moon
The band that Marion leads
The glitter of their rifles,
The scampering of their steeds
'Tis life to guide the fiery bark
Across the moonlight plain;
'Tis life to feel the night wind
That lifts the tossing mane.
A moment in the British camp—
A moment—and away
Back to the pathless forest
Before the peep of day.

Grave men there are by broad pantee,
Grave men with hoary hairs;
Their hearts are all with Marion,
For Marion are their prayers.
And lovely ladies greet our band
With kindliest welcoming,
With smiles like those of summer
And tears like those of spring.
For them we wear these trusty arms
And lay them down no more
Till we have driven the Briton,
Forever, from our shore

William Bryant

The Swamp Fox at Black Mingo Bridge

Francis Marion of South Carolina has been compared to Robin Hood for emerging from the wilds to administer justice. In fact, it is said that because of his ability to pop in and out of the wildwood when least expected, Marion's foes labeled him "Swamp Fox."

The year 1780 was probably the most eventful one in the struggle for independence in South Carolina. In early September 1780, British forces were actively moving into the Williamsburg area. This activity was largely due to the fact that Lord Cornwallis was preparing for a major effort to secure British operations in North and South Carolina, and the forces of Francis Marion posed a definite threat to the British stronghold at Georgetown.

Colonel Balfour, commander of English forces at Charlestown ordered Major James Moncrieff and battalion of the Seventh Regiment of Georgetown. The loyalist militia commanded by Col. John Coming Ball and Col. Joseph Wigfal had also been called into Georgetown. And, in a final attempt to purge the area of insurrection, Major James Wemyss was ordered to lead the Sixty-Third Regiment, reinforced by Lt. Col. John Hamilton's loyalist militia, into Williamsburg.

Following Cornwallis's order "to put a good face on things," Wemyss desolated the country between Black River and Lynches River, an area seventy miles long and as much as fifteen miles wide. Homes were plundered and burned, livestock was killed and provisions were destroyed.

It was during this invasion was burned as a "sedition shop." Marion's amazing intelligence network reported that resistance was hopeless—it was obvious that his forces were for outnumbered.

Allowing most and leaving Major James and ten hand-picked men to gather information, Marion fled with a few men to the Great White Marsh on the Waccamaw River in North Carolina.

Marion's men did not fare well. About ten days had passed by the time Major James arrived at the Great White Marsh to find many of his compatriots suffering from malaria. This situation was compounded by the news he brought to the destruction wrought by Wemyss. However, Major James also reported that the "wantonness and cruelty" of Weymess and his command had so enraged the population that many men were ready to take the field. Marion decided to make his move. On September 24, 1780, Marion broke camp.

Early in the evening on September 28, his troops had reached Whitherspoon's Ferry on Lynches River where they were joined by Capt. James and his ten men, Cap. Henry Mouzon, Lt. Joseph Scott and some of the militia. Some of Marion's group was near exhaustion but "finding his men unanimous for battle, he gratified their wishes." They headed for Black Mingo.

Colonel John Coming Ball with approximately fifty men had moved from Georgetown and camped at the Red house, the tavern of Patrick Dollard. At this strategic point near Shepherd's Ferry on Black Mingo, the Tories could control traffic on the creek as well as the post road which passed nearby. Ball was also close enough to Kingstree and Indiantown to move his troops if the need arose.

After weeks of futile pursuit, the Tories gave up trying to catch the Swamp Fox, and he advanced southward. Information reached him that the enemy force was stationed on the Black Mingo Creek, and he determined to surprise and capture their camp. The only approach to it was over a plank bridge. Unfortunately, the galloping hooves of the horses as they crossed were heard through the stillness of the night, and an alarm gun warned the sleeping Tories of his approach. He withdrew and put socks on his horses' hooves. Marion then ordered a charge, and the patriots swept down on the enemy with irresistible fury. The Tories fled in confusion, and their commander was killed. The surprise and the capture were complete. It is said that after the conflict Marion never crossed a bridge at night without first having his men spread blankets upon it to deaden the sound.

The swamps were alive with animals, some wild, but also those that escaped the devastation of Tories who burned, stole, raped, and destroyed their way across the country. The cattle were looking for food and it was brother against brother.

The Swamp Fox—he was watchful cautious, suspicious, and travelled by the night and he was at home in the swamps; the best known was Snow's Island. Yes, he was a fox. He's hit them run so he could fight another day. He didn't fight clean; he fought to win. Brutal, he looted, murdered, burned, and stole and was at times unappreciated. He was a shadowy figure using guerilla warfare. He and his wigs stood alone against the British in lower South Carolina.

Pending the predatory warfare of Hamilton in Williamsburg, a party of marauding Tories went to the house of Captain William Gordon and commenced plundering the house. But conscience makes men cowards. The alarm was given, whether false or not, does not appear that the Whigs were coming when the whole party fled. One of them becoming fastened some way in the fence was unable to get over. Mrs. Gordon ran and caught the fellow and pulling him down her side of the fence detained him until help came and he was secured."

At another time, the freebooters came and carried off all Mr. Gordon's horses while he was absent fighting the battles of his country. Mrs. Gordon, unable to prevent the robbery, followed the party at a distance and observed where the horses were enclosed. That night when went alone, caught the best horse in the lot-better than any of her own and mounting him-rode away in safety with her reprisal."

Boddie relates that Margaret learned of Cornwallis's preparation to send Tarleton after Marion and set out alone on horseback for Snow's Island from her home just east of Camden, a forty mile journey, arriving the same day. She related her story to Marion after which he "secured a large comfortable tent for her and ordered for her a roast wild turkey dinner and a bottle of Horry's rare Italian wine." The following day a strong guard accompanied her home.

Colonel Doyle, commanding the "Invincible Irish" regiment of regulars, a fresh regiment of regulars from New York which had just arrived at Camden from Charles Town tow independent commands of Tory Calvary, between two and three hundred men each, and some smaller Tory commands all of these troops mounted was ordered to cross the Pee Dee on its western reaches and proceed eastward along its northern bank and to come down on Snow's Island at the same time Watson came from the south. These two armies were to drive the Swamp Fox into his den and to dig him out.

For the next incident, I will quote directly from Boddie: "Mrs. Margaret Gordon, wife of Captain William Gordon of Marion's brigade, learned of these plans while they were being discussed in Camden and as soon as she believed she had the essentials she made three copies of the plans as she had heard them and sent them by three of Marion's trustworthy scouts which had been stationed on the Gordon Plantation for such a purpose. Mrs. Gordon gave each of them a fast horse and told them to 'ride' which in the parlance of that time and place, meant to proceed as rapidly as possible. General Marion read the paper the scouts delivered and had his bugler sound assembly summoning every man on the island to his headquarters. He had been expecting some such move against him ever since Greene and Lee had left and his plans had all been made."

Marion sent out immediately his scouts along every road and trail from Snow's Island. They were sounding the summons "every man comes immediately with as much food as practical, but every man must come now." At the same time he sent a special messenger to his old friend John Nesmith, asking him to send him ten beefs dressed.

Skirmish at Black Mingo Creek

September 14, 1780, General Marion's troops routed the Tories under Captain J. Coming Ball, attacked on one flank by Captain Thomas Waites and on the other by Colonel Horry with General Marion's reserves in rear. The Tories fled into Black Mingo Swamp through of short duration. The action was so sharply contested that each side lost nearly one third of its men. Killed and wounded,

Captain Henry Mouzon and Lieutenant Joseph Scott were both wounded there, and were carried to White Marsh in North Carolina where they remained until their recovery. You could say when the war really began brothers and sisters gathered for church, weddings and fellowship. All of a sudden, they were enemies-burning, looting, killing each other.

The American Revolutionary War, On October 7, 1780, The Battle of Kings Mountain was fought, sparking the series of events that eventually led to England's loss of America. The situation for the rebellious colonies looked bleak in 1778. In attempting to end the war, the British had turned their efforts to the South, launching a full-scale invasion in the autumn of 1778.

By 1780 the British controlled Georgia and had won important victories at Charleston and Camden. Lord Cornwallis, British commander in the South, believed that South Carolina was won. Turning his attention to North Carolina, he began to march from Charleston. Cornwallis hoped to invade North Carolina at Charlotte by September. One of his officers, Major Patrick Ferguson, was to move through the up country of South Carolina border, wiping out patriot, resistance and protecting the flank and rear of Cornwallis' advancing army.

After moving across the western North Carolina border, Ferguson established his base at Gilbert Town, today the site of Rutherfordton. Ferguson underestimated the local people and their desire to take up arms against the British. He threatened to "hang their leaders and to lay their country to waste with fire and sword." Rather than cowering, the citizens stiffened their opposition. A call went out to mobilize against the hated British.

On September 25 at Sycamore Shoals near the present town of Elizabethton, Tennessee, more than a thousand volunteers assembled. The next day, the famous march over the mountains began. Meanwhile, Ferguson had been warned of the formidable force that was being organized against him. Unknown to the patriots, Ferguson left Gilbert Town heading toward Ninety-Six. He also sent an urgent to Cornwallis asking for reinforcements. Unfortunately for Ferguson, his message did not reach Cornwallis until after the battle.

Instead of marching to Ninety-Six, Ferguson hastened toward Charlotte, North Carolina, hoping that the patriots would not learn of his diversionary move. The American patriot force reached Gilbert Town on October 4. Learning that Ferguson and his troops were no longer there, the patriots took after the British in hot pursuit. The patriots were fortunate volunteers, bringing the total to 1,800 fighting men. At Cowpens a select group of the toughest fighting in the patriotic force was chosen to overtake Ferguson. After an exhausting overland march, the patriots arrived near Kings Mountain on October.

The Battle of Kings Mountain lasted only about an hour and resulted in a complete victory for the patriots. The British relied on the bayonet. The patriots relied on their marksmanship and the deadly accuracy of their Kentucky rifles. After withstanding several bayonet charges by the British, the patriots surrounded and disorganized the enemy. Ferguson made one futile attempt to rally his troops but was shot dead by sharpshooters. The British surrendered.

The patriots' surprising and devastating victory at Kings Mountain changed the course of the Revolutionary War. The immediate result was the delay of Cornwallis' northward march and the abandonment of his stronghold at Charlotte. The morale of the patriots was boosted, resistance to the British increased, and the patriotic forces began to take the offensive.

Halfway Swamp and Singleton's Mill

After camping near Thomas Sumter's house on the Santee and failing to engage Francis Marion's militia, Major Robert McLeroth was frustrated, and his superior officers were losing patience with him. In December 1781, McLeroth and his men of the Sixth-Fourth Regiment were ordered to conduct raw new recruits for the Royal Fusiliers towards the High Hills.

Learning from his spies that the recruits had marched from Charleston, Marion issued a call for the militia to assemble. Times were slack and most men were idle, and so they came trooping in. When Marion marched towards Nelson's Ferry, he had seven horsemen at his back. They marched across Williamsburg and up the Santee Road. By December 12, they had passed Nelson's Ferry and just above half way swamp, some miles above the ferry, they overtook the unsuspecting Major McLeroth.

Marion immediately dispatched riflemen to skirmish with the rear guard. Then, wheeling his horsemen around McLeroth's flank, he began a direct attack. McLeroth's men and the recruits scrambled into a field enclosed by a rail fence, posting themselves behind the fence jams to fire on the horsemen. Marion's men moved to the shore of a dark, boggy cypress pond and waited. Soon McLeroth sent an officer under a flag of truce. The officer upbraided Marion for attacking the rear guard, contrary, he said, to all the laws of civilized warfare, and challenged Marion's men to come out of the woods and fight in the open field. Citing Wemyss and Tarleton, Marion replied that burning the houses of Whigs was worse than shooting armed guards. "I consider the challenge that of a man in desperate circumstances," he said. "But if Major McLeroth wishes to see mortal combat between teams of twenty men picked by each side, I will gratify him."

McLeroth accepted. The two sides agreed to a battleground near an old oak tree in the field, and each commanding officer chose twenty sharpshooters. Marion chose Major John Vanderhorst to command his team. Vanderhorst's men agreed to advance to within fifty yards of the British as the surest distance to strike with buckshot. Vanderhorst told the team that after he gave the signal, "each man will fire at the one directly opposite of him, and on my word few will be left for a second shot."

As the Whig sharpshooters closed to fifty yards, an officer passed hurriedly along the enemy line. At his command the British shouldered their muskets and retreated. After giving three cheers, Vanderhorst and his men returned to their comrades.

McLeroth likely had no intention of wasting good troops in such an encounter. Rather, he was stalling for more time to get his men out of a bad situation. As soon as he had seen Marion's advance guard, he had sent couriers racing for help. They met Captain John Coffin and one hundred in forty Loyalists, mounted infantrymen of the New York Volunteers sent to escort the recruits. But instead of coming to McLeroth's rescue, Coffin turned back and lodged his troops behind Swift Creek. As Lord Rawdon, the British commander at Camden, advised Cornwallis: "Information was given Coffin that he was to be attacked in the night and a large body of the Enemy approached very near him in the evening. Under these circumstances, Coffin judged it best to retire."

Race to Singleton's Mill

So McLeroth tried another tactic. During the night his troops shouted and sang around huge campfires. Then, around midnight, with the fires still burning, they abandoned their supplies and slipped away on the road to Singleton's Mill, some ten miles north. At daylight Marion discovered the ruse. Immediately he dispatched Major Hugh Horry and a hundred horsemen to beat McLeroth to Singleton's. Realizing that he couldn't overtake him, Horry detached Major John James and a group with the fastest horses to ride around the millpond and seize Singleton's houses.

James outraced the British to Matthew Singleton's property, two hundred acres mostly of rich swampland, with dams and ponds for rice cultivation, creeks, and a grist mill. James circled around the millpond and swept up the hill to the house just as McLeroth's men reached the foot. James' men seized the buildings and delivered one shot before they realized that the Singletons were sick with smallpox. As quickly as they had come, the Whigs abandoned the buildings and left them to the British. The next day Marion moved his men back down the Santee Road, and soon Coffin joined McLeroth at Singleton's Mill. But neither McLeroth nor Coffin pursued Marion. With the engagements ended in a draw and Marion at large, McLeroth's military career was coming to an end. "I must immediately dislodge Marion," Rawdon informed Cornwallis on December 17. "But as McLeroth has not quite enterprise enough, I shall let him go to Charleston (which he wishes)."

McLeroth's Character

While the British commanders in South Carolina were dissatisfied with McLeroth's performance in the field, several Whig sources attest to his uprightness and generosity. Major William Dobein James, who rode with Marion during the chase, wrote, "It has been currently reported that he carried his dislike of house burning so far, that he neglected to carry into effect the orders of his commander-in-chief on that point to such an extent as to gain his ill will and that of many other British officers."

Peter Horry recounted that during the skirmishing between Halfway Swamp and Singleton's Mill, after each side had several wounded, McLeroth left them in a tavern under a flag of truce. There he had stationed a physician and paid for two weeks' lodging for the wounded. When Marion arrived at the tavern, the old woman who ranit begged him not to harm McLeroth. "For," she said, "he's the sweetest-spoken, mildest-looking, noblest-spirited Englishman I ever saw in my born days."

After leaving the tavern, Marion rode a long while in silence. Then he turned to Horry and said, "Well, I suppose I feel now very much as I would in pursuit of a brother to kill him."

Horry remarked in his account, "From the effect produced on our troops, by this admirable officer's conduct, I have often been led to think favorably of a saying common with Marion: 'Had the British officers but acted as became a wise and magnanimous enemy, they might easily have recovered the revolted colonies."

Even Lord Rawdon admitted the effect of McLeroth's behavior. He sent Major John Campbell to the High Hills of Santee to take control of McLeroth's regiment, but reported secretly to Cornwallis: "In justice to McLeroth, I should mention that his mild and equitable behavior to the inhabitants of that country has been of great service."

Troops marched through every area of the state—two hundred battles and skirmishes. Nine occurred in Georgetown County—Black Mingo, September 28–29, 1780; Black River Road., October 9, 1780; Sampit Road, November 20, 1780; White's Plantation, December 28, 1780; Waccamaw Neck, January 14, 1781; Georgetown, January 25, 1781; February 21, 1781; May 28, 1781; and August 2, 1781.

His brother, Gabriel, once owned Laurel Hill, one of four plantations that made up what today is Brookgreen Gardens. During the four years that elapsed from the Battle of Fort Moultrie to the surrender of Charleston, Georgetown flourished on wartime trade, although the dangers of the sea became increasingly dangerous.

South Carolina Governor John Rutledge, who fled the Holy City before the capture of Charleston, was in Georgetown on May 5 to rally the people to defend the ferry landings along the Santee. On July 1, Captain John Plumer Ardesoif captured Georgetown from the sea, and sent sailors in armed barges up the rivers to plunder the plantations. On July 11, Wemyss arrived with the Sixty-Third Royal Regiment to take command of Georgetown.

On September 28, 1780, Marion and his men aroused by the savagery of Wemyss successfully attacked the loyalists' militia at Black Mingo, in western Georgetown County. This would not be the last time the British felt Marion's sting in Georgetown. Shortly before the year ended, on December 28, another skirmish occurred on the Black River Ferry Road between Marion's men and a British patrol.

Lieutenant Colonel George Campbell was the commanding officer at Georgetown when 1781 arrived. Campbell was greeted by an English garrison that contained 300 men and had the pesky Swamp Fox, steadily knocking at the door.

On January 14, near Brookgreen Plantation, a small group of Marion's men under command of Colonel Peter Horry encountered about twenty British soldiers who were foraging for the salt. A brief skirmish took place and the British retreated with Horry giving chase. Horry came face-to-face with Campbell and about sixty of his men. Overwhelmed, Horry was obliged to retreat, but not before he captured two dragoons. That was the lone skirmish fought on the Waccamaw Neck during the war.

On January 23, Marion whose guerrilla militia was bolstered by the arrival of Light Horse Harry Lee and continentals, sent men down the Pee Dee to hide among the rice fields while his militia and Lee's legion landed in the watery suburbs of the town. They attacked Georgetown on the night of January 24. The surprise worked and Campbell was captured, but most of the British troops remained barricaded in the brick fort, which, without battering and scaling equipment and without artillery, could not be penetrated.

The next month, on February 21, a small party of Marion's men captured British Captain Fames De Peyster and 25 British soldiers who had been detached on service a few miles from Georgetown. On May 23, the British evacuated Georgetown just five days before Marion launched another attack against the fortification. While the British hovered in sight of the mouth of Winyah Bay, Marion leveled the fortifications.

It was estimated that 2,500 men served under Marion at one time or another. Most of his men were drawn from the small farmers who lived along the Black and Pee Dee rivers, or from the Scotch-Irish of the Black Mingo region. Throughout the war, the South Carolina farmers in the untrained militia proved to be every bit as effective as the well-schooled American troops they fought alongside. The Marion led militia held the point position in the Battle of Eutaw Springs on September 8, 1781, where the British suffered the highest percentage of losses of any battle in the war. Of about two thousand British troops, eighty-five were killed, 350 were wounded, and four hundred were listed as missing.

Isaac Hayne

One of the prominent South Carolinians who took up arms against Great Britain was Isaac Hayne (1745-1781), a prosperous young planter and businessman from St. Bartholomew Parish on the Edisto. Married and the father of seven children, Hayne owned three large plantations in St. Bartholomew's as well as city lots in Beaufort and Charleston and extensive holdings in Georgia and the Carolina Piedmont. He kept extensive records of the births, deaths and sales of his hundreds of African slaves, most of who grew indigo that was known in the province for its high quality. In the New Acquisition District (today's York County] he was partner with William Hill in the Area Furnace, an "iron plantation" where slaves forged household goods and firearms for retail and wholesale trade. According to their agreement, Hill built and supervised the furnace, while Hayne supplied the slaves both for the ironwork and for the farm that supported the entire operation. Like most young men of his class, Hayne was active in South Carolina politics. Before the break with Great

Britain he served in the Commons House of Assembly and on a commission charged with raising money to build courthouse and jails; under the revolutionary government he was elected to the House of Representatives and then to the Senate. When South Carolina Whigs took up arms against the King, the Area Furnace supplied the militias with military hardware.

Except where otherwise noted, this account is based on the narrative of Robert D. Bass:

Militia Leader:

When Sir Henry Clinton invaded South Carolina in early 1780, Isaac Hayne was among the low country citizens who took up arms to defend the capital city. Hayne raised a troop of cavalry and was soon appointed Commandant of the Colleton County Regiment. In May, after Charleston fell to the British, the South Carolina militiamen were "permitted to return to their respective homes as prisoner on parole," and Hayne returned to his plantation. The next month, Clinton revoked the paroles and demanded that former rebels affirm their allegiance to the King or face appropriation of their properties. Hayne, like many Whigs, had little choice but to accept Clinton's conditions. As long as the British held the low country, Hayne felt bound by his oath and turned down Gen. Marion's invitation to command a Whig militia regiment.

By the winter of 1780–1781, the situation had changed remarkably. Constant harassment by Pickens, Sumter, and Marion and the arrival of an army of Continentals under Gen. Nathaniel Greene had left the British in firm control only of Charleston and its immediate environs. Away from the city, Whig sympathizers who had taken the oath of allegiance began to take up arms again. William Harden, a planter from the backcountry between Beaufort and Augusta (today's Barnwell County), attempted to raise a regiment in the southernmost portion of the province. He visited Marion, received commissions for his officers and began recruiting. Harden was able to raise a considerable force, but he found that the Whigs along the Edisto River, led by Isaac Hayne, were still reluctant to join him. In April

1781, Harden successfully attacked Tory forces at Four Holes and Fort Balfour. Pursued by Maj. Thomas Fraser's dragoons, he retreated into the swamps below the Salkehatchie. "I am obliged to haul off southwardly to collect all the men I can in those parts," he reported to Marion on April 18. With a couple of minor victories behind him, Harden planned to renew his recruiting along the Edisto. He requested some blank officer commissions and hoped that enticing Hayne back into service would convince his neighbors:

I beg you will send some immediately with your orders, it seems they wait for Col. Hayne's, and he says he can't without a Commission, and is sure, if he turns out, that at least two hundred will join him, if so, I am very sure that this part of the country may be held. Marion sent the commissions. With the British in retreat, Hayne felt he was released from his prior obligations to the British and finally organized a regiment.

On June 5, Hayne led a small squadron of horsemen to the outskirts of Charleston and captured Andrew Williamson, a distinguished backcountry Whig who had fled to British lines and was widely assumed to have turned traitor. Col. Balfour sent Maj. Thomas Fraser and ninety dragoons in pursuit of Hayne's party. Fraser captured Hayne in uniform, bearing arms, and in command of Whig militiamen—from the British perspective, in clear violation of his oath of allegiance. Balfour decided to make an example of him. For three weeks he held him in the provost dungeon, the basement prison of the Exchange Building. Then, on July 27, he ordered Hayne brought before a court of field officers "in order to determine under what point of view you ought to be considered." Major Andrew McKenzie, a loyalist, presided, and the prisoner appeared without counsel. The court met again the next evening. They properly identified Hayne, confirmed the circumstances of his capture, and then turned their findings over to the two senior officers. Balfour and Rawdon, "in consequence of the most express direction of Lord Cornwallis to us, that all those who should be found in arms, after being at their own request received as subjects" of Britain, ordered that Hayne be hanged. He went to the gallows on August 4, the most prominent American to be executed for treason during the Revolutionary War.

Parker's Ferry

Following Hayne's execution, the ranks of the Whig militia began to decline, while the Tories were emboldened. Balfour sent Fraser and his dragoons into the territory south of the Edisto to assist the Tory militiamen. Marion and two hundred of his men were under orders from General Greene to help harden in his effort to keep the British from St. Stevens to meet Fraser. On August 30, 1781, learning that Fraser's men were returning to the Edisto, Marion decided to ambush them on the causeway leading to Parker's Ferry. From a distance of fifty yards his men opened fire with buckshot. The entire line of dragoons reeled, men falling, horses screaming and rearing. Fraser rallied his horsemen and tried to charge into the swamp, but Marion's men had time to fire a second and third volley, killing perhaps a hundred men before the remainder could flee.

Now begins the active part of his Revolutionary career. On June 21, 1775, he was commissioned as captain in the Second Regiment under Colonel William Moultrie, his captain in the Cherokee War. In the same regiment, Captain Peter Horry received his commission. They were to see each other often. Captain Marion was a born soldier. He never required of others more than he was willing to do himself. He trained his men to a degree of military skill that made them all proud. In the Pee Dee, a small group of wigs gathered in the swamps. Marion asked and received permission to organize and lead them. The number of men ranged from forty to two hundred, according to the time of year. They lived off of what they could find. The women of the district were his dependable aids in all things, but especially in furnishing him information. Many of the women in the district at this time could ride horses as well as their brothers could. They looked to Marion for protection, and they gave him all they could.

General Marion made his headquarters on Snows Island. From that point, he conducted his campaigns throughout eastern Carolina. It has been said of him that he was never beaten, never surprised, and it has been said that he has never made a serious military mistake.

In March 1776, the second regiment under Colonel Moultrie was ordered to take post on Sullivan's Island at the entrance to the Charles Town Harbor. The British fleet consisted of nine vessels. Of these, two were fifty gunships, five carried twenty – eight guns each, and one carried twenty guns. The other was a bomb vessel. On June 20, these vessels anchored before the fort that Francis Marion and his men had been sent to secure. They had a scarcity of ammunition, but the British ships moved out of range of Marion's gunfire, and Francis Marion himself had the last shot! After that brilliant defense of Fort Sullivan, not much is heard of Captain Francis Marion for a few years.

Mr. Meredith Hughes was a loyalist, and his son was a Whig. When the American ties with Britain began to break, the first provincial congress of South Carolina emerged and designated an association in 1775, which bound Carolinians to fight if bound by Congress. The association organized the first and second regiments. Of the first eight captains elected, six were from Georgetown. During the time between the Battle of Moultrie and the Siege of Charleston in 1780, Georgetown flourished on wartime trade. However, the period of calm was ended when Charleston surrendered. Lord Cornwallis, the British commander in the south, knew that he must have control of the back country as well as the coastal towns if he was to out the fire of insurrection that was burning.

The British entered Georgetown on July 1, 1780. They captured the town and went up the rivers on plundering expeditions. This angered the men in these areas and hereby started a new rebellion. At this time, a great militia leader, by the name of Francis Marion, began to emerge. Marion was born in St John's Parish, Berkley, and he was at Belle Isle near Georgetown. One of Marion's first important skirmishes in Georgetown County came at Shepard's Ferry over Black Mingo creek. Major James Moncrief, in constructing Georgetown's defenses, placed Colonel John Coming Ball near Patrick Dallard's Tavern at Shepard's Ferry. Marion came upon Colonel Ball's loyal militia during one night in September 1780 and routed them in fifteen minutes. Some of Marion's officers were the rice planting class, but the majority of his men were the small farmers who lived along the Black River and Pee Dee River and the Black Mingo Creek. It was very important from a military standpoint to the British that they should crush this Williamsburg spirit. The British sent Tarleton through Williamsburg, but Tarleton was too chivalrous a foe to do the destructive work the British authorities deemed necessary, so, a few days later, Lord Cornwallis sent Major Wemyss through Williamsburg to do the work that Tarleton had left undone.

Major Wemyss crossed Black River on the west side at Benbow's Ferry on the western boundary of Williamsburg on August 20, 1780, and destroyed all the dwelling houses, cattle, and sheep in that community. Wemyss laid waste a tract of country between Black River and the Pee Dee River seventy miles in length and in some places, fifteen miles wide. On August 27, 1780, Major James met him and killed fifteen of his men and took a number of prisoners. Wemyss withdrew and hurried on the Indiantown road to Georgetown. Wemyss burned the Indiantown Church. In August 1780, Marion's Brigade was the only body of American troops in South Carolina. Williamsburg and Francis Marion alone stood in the way of complete domination in South Carolina. The Georgetown and Camden roads by way of Black Mingo to Kingstree ran through the heart of Williamsburg. The British planned to establish a chain of strongholds. One of these strongholds along this road, which the British strategists had planned, was about twenty miles on the way from Georgetown to Kingstree on Black Mingo Creek. The British proceeded up Black River and a short distance up the Black Mingo to Patrick Dollard's Inn, known as the "Red House," just south of Shepard's Ferry. The British made this Red House Headquarters.

Taken From *The Life of General Francis Marion* by Brigadier General P. Horry and Parson M. L. Weems:

Carolina apparently lost—Marion almost alone keeps the field—begins to figure—surprises a strong British party at Nelson's old field—scourges the Tories at Black Mingo—Witherspoon's Ferry at Lynches River—again smites them hip and high on Pee Dee.

Indigo fields grew into wild wood. During the Revolution, the large herds of cattle that fed and flourished along the swamps and creeks and rivers emptying into Black River had either been exhausted in supplying Marion's men with beef or wantonly destroyed during the several British campaigns in this district.

"Major John James of Indiantown was the son of William James and Elizabeth Witherspoon, and as a baby boy had accompanied his parents to Williamsburg in the first colony. He was the representative of the township in the state legislature and had received a captaincy by royal appointment, but had thrown up his commission at the beginning of the revolution, saying he would never fight for a tyrant. To his, as a leader of Williamsburg, may be ascribed much of the credit for the forming of Marion's Brigade and the consequent victorious struggle made by South Carolina to throw off the conqueror's yoke.

"Major James was selected by the people of Williamsburg to investigate proclamation posted by a British naval officer at Georgetown calling on South Carolinians to swear allegiance to the King and secure protection, which many Georgetown citizens had done.

"Dressed not as a captain of the Royal Army but in the plain clothes of a planter, Major James saddled his black Arabian steed, Thunder, and rode to Georgetown to interview Ardesoif, the British officer. On being told that not only submission but service in arms for the King would be required of South Carolinians, James replied, 'The people I represent would never submit to those terms.'

"Ardesoif drew his sword, advanced threateningly and said, 'You damn rebel! I shall have you hung at my yard arm.' Whereupon John James, unarmed, picked up his chair, kept it between Ardesoif and himself while he escaped out the door. Leaping upon his horse, which he had prudently hitched near the door, he sped away down the old trail cut by the forty first settlers from Georgetown to Kingstree. We can almost hear the flying hoof-beats of that high-spirited steed as it bore its equally high-spirited master back to report the insult to his people.

"When the incident was told that night and quickly repeated throughout the district, the clans assembled at the King's Tree to organize for liberty. They gathered near our present court house square, those fiery Scots-Irish, three hundred strong.

The Ervins, Scotts, Burgesses, Dickeys, Friesons, Nelsons, McClarys, Montgomerys and Campbells came with Henry Mouzon of Pudding Swamp, captain of the King's Tree militia.

"From south of Black River, the Gambles, McGills, Friersons, Watsons, Boyds, Gordons and Whitherspoons came and chose John Macauley their captain.

"From Lynch's Lake, the Jameses, McBrides, McCallisters, Matthews, Haseldons, McFaddens, and Rogers called John James of the lake to command their company.

"From Ceadere Swamp and Black Mingo, the McCants, McConnells, McCulloughs, McKnights, McCreas, McCutchens and Nesmiths made Robert McCottry their captain.

"These four Scots-Irish companies thus organized, elected Major James their commander. But Major James, fully aware of the clannish loyalties of the Scottish battalion, wisely felt a complete stranger could best lead this fiery body of men through the perils of war. Hence he dispatched a message to Gen. Gates requesting that Francis Marion be sent to take the leadership. Until Marion arrived, James yielded the command to Marion's bosom friend, Col. Hugh Horry, who came to strengthen the Williamsburg battalion.

"Thus came into being Marion's Brigade, which was never beaten and never surprised. After Tarleton had temporarily scattered Sumter's Legion and Baron de Kalbhad fallen in the Battle of Camden, in which the militia under General Gates was scattered by Cornwallis, Williamsburg and Francis Marion were alone unconquered in South Carolina.

"Marion's Brigade, of which he was later made general, consisted of uncertain numbers. Sometimes there were only a dozen in the band, but always they were Marion's Men. Clad often in the skins of animals which they trapped, they lived in the swamps of the district for more than two years. Their food was fish, game, berries, sweet potatoes, or whatever they could find. Sometimes they helped themselves boldly to the supplies of the enemy. Brought up on horseback herding wild cattle in Williamsburg swamps, expert as marksmen from lifelong experience as huntsmen, Marion's men had the endurance and courage of pioneer woodsmen. Such qualities made soldiers who overcame by valor their tragic lack of gunpowder. Their swords were filed out of handsaws by the people of the community. Their bullets sometimes were pewter spoons and cups melted in the hearth fire by their brave women.

"The scarcity of ammunition forced Marion to avoid engagements in open battle. Often his men had no more than two rounds of shot. From his retreat at Snow's Island, in the Pee Dee swamps at Lynch's Creek, or some other dry island hidden in the swampy morass, Marion's men would sally forth by the light of the moon to pester the British outposts. Like will-o'-wisps, they tempted their enemy into the swamps, always just beyond their grasp.

"The devil himself could not capture that Swamp Fox and his web-footed troops,' said Tarleton after his unsuccessful campaign against Marion in Williamsburg.

"Tarleton's invasion of Williamsburg occurred soon after the mobilization of the Scots-Irish. At the head of his red-coated cavalry and his Tories in Civilian clothes, Tarleton entered Williamsburg over the Santee River at Lenud's Ferry to surprise Major James. But Captain McCottry, with a force of fifty riflemen was advanced by the Major to rout Tarleton at his encampment at Kingstree. Tarleton was informed by the wife of John Hamilton, one of the few Tories in Williamsburg, had marched away, to be pursued by the intrepid Kingstree company.

"Routed by the patriots, Tarleton avenged himself by burning to the ground the dwelling and outhouse of Capt. [Henry] Mouzon, fourteen buildings in all in spite of the pleas of Mrs. Mouzon and her children. The homes of William and Edward Plowden were also burned, and the aged James Bradley, an original settler, taken prisoner and kept in chains at Camden for the duration of the war.

"Except for sharp encounters with the Tories, Tarleton's invasion began the bloodshed that made of all Williamsburg a battlefield. The second attempt to community at Benbow's Ferry on Black River, setting fire to the homes of Maj. John Gamble, Capt. James Conyers, James Davis, Capt. John Nelson, Robert Frierson, John Frierson, Robert Gamble and William Gamble as he approached. He also burned Indiantown church and the homes of Maj. John James besides destroying loom-house and sheep. Had the corn crop been gathered, famine would have stalked in his wake. Salt was then ten dollar a bushel, and even at that price was difficult to obtain. Property destroyed could not be replaced and the people could be seen after the fires searching for knife-blades, scissors, hinges and nails. Dishes and plates were rudely fashioned of wood,' and the inhabitants assisted one another in building log huts to replace their burned homes. Most of this dastardly destruction was perpetrated by Harrison's Tories.

"After the desolation left by Wemyss, Marion Brigade was strengthened by hundreds of volunteers anxious to avenge the wrongs. The Swamp Fox hurried back from North Carolina, where he had been forced to retreat before Wemyss to prevent the wholesale destruction of his small unequipped troops by overwhelming odds. Preparations were then made to protect Williamsburg against the third invasion of the British under Col. Watson.

"The enemy was met at Wiboo Swamp where occurred the famous deed of the immense Gavin James who held in check and faced the volleys of the entire British force.

"In this invasion also was recorded the heroic defense of the Lower Bridge, not far from this spot, by Maj. James and Capt. McCottry, commanding men who were fighting almost in sight of their homes. The deadly marksmanship of McCottry's Kingstree riflemen has passed into history. With Marion's directing them, the men of Williamsburg drove the enemy into Georgetown.

"Such were Marion's men, who kept alive the struggle for freedom when the courage of South Carolina was at its lowest ebb; Marion's men, to whom may be ascribed the turning of the tide that ended in liberty for South Carolina and the young United Stated.

There is scarcely a name in Williamsburg that boasts not a part in that record; there is scarcely a spot in Williamsburg not arced to some deed of heroism!

"See Brittania's hosts retreating,
Proud no more of victories won;
Hear Columbia's sons repeating
Loud the name of WASHINGTON
Carolina's son repeating
HORRY, JAMES AND MARION.'

"By forced of overwhelming numbers, superior equipment and unlimited means, the British finally conquered Charleston in 1780. The ragged South Carolina troops were captured; and the city, then the capital of the state, was taken possession of by the foe, who felt confident that the state was subdued and would remain a British colony.

"The men of Williamsburg had marched down to the defense of the capital and upon its surrender were made prisoners of war and allowed to return home on parole. Many citizens of the state thus submitted as prisoners of war in order to be permitted to go about their affairs and be with their families. The spirit of the state was apparently broken. South Carolina might in truth have remained a British possession had it not been for the patriots of Williamsburg and Francis Marion.

"By fortuitous circumstances, neither Marion, then a colonel, nor Major John James of Williamsburg were taken prisoner at the fall of Charlestown. When the city surrendered, Marion was at home on leave because of a broken ankle, and Major James had been ordered back by Governor Rutledge to train the militia in the district between the Santee and Pee Dee.

Marion at Port's Ferry

In September 1780, Francis Marion was encamped at Port's Ferry where, among the ardent Whigs of Britton's Neck, he was relatively secure. While he waited there for Peter Horry to join him, Francis Goddard and his half-brothers Samuel and Britton Jenkins, sons of the Revolutionary War heroine the Widow Jenkins, joined his little band.

Northeast on Catfish Creek, along Little Pee Dee and up the branches of Drowning Creek were many people who felt they had little in common with the Low Country and were still loyal to the King of England. They had formed a regiment of Loyalist militia under the command of Major Micajah Ganey, with Jesse Barefield as second in command. Allied with the British invaders, these Tories were as dangerous as the redcoats themselves. Receiving word that Marion was camping at Port's Ferry, Ganey called out his militia—250 men—to the mustering field on Little Pee Dee. Since Marion kept his scouts moving and listening, he was not to be caught by surprise. With only 52 men, however, what should be his course of action?

He rejected the idea of running and decided to attack first. Before daylight on September 4, Marion was up and riding from Port's Ferry to surprise the Tories who were up and preparing to surprise him at Port's Ferry. His Brigade first scattered Ganey's horsemen and then pursued the Tory infantry under Barefield into the Blue Savannah morass. In these two skirmishes, at a cost of four men wounded and two horses killed, he broke the power of the Tories east of the Pee Dee.

Almost immediately afterwards, sixty volunteers rode into his camp, and with his forces doubled, Marion began to fortify his retreat to protect the Ferry, "awe the Tories," and blockade the post road that ran from Savannah to Boston, he threw up a redoubt of logs and clay and behind the ramparts mounted two small cannon. They pointed along the road and across the river as guardians of the area's liberty.

Finally in 1782, after the British strategy collapsed at Yorktown, Marion had the satisfaction of watching the British army sail away for England. The Revolution had ended in victory for the Americans, and Francis Marion's grueling war with the British became history. After the war, Marion finally married. He retained a command in the state militia and served in the state senate. His last years, however, were spent at his cherished plantation experimenting with methods of growing indigo. There, in the heart of the South Carolina Low Country he had fought so hard to protect, the old soldier died quietly on February 26, 1795, at the age of sixty-three.

Another chapter in the ferry's history unfolded after the Revolutionary War with Methodist Bishop Francis Asbury's missionary journeys into South Carolina. The first of these began in February 1785 and continued until his last journey in 1816. One of his favorite routes brought him to Cheraw, thence to Port's Ferry, Witherspoon's Black Mingo, Black River, and Georgetown, where he turned towards Charlestown. In his journals he notes at least seven times that he spent at Port's Ferry, preaching nearby. On his 1811 journey, he writes, "Found Mother Port keeping house at eighty-seven rafts and boats in quantities passing down the Pee Dee." The influence of Francis Asbury on the religious and social life of the backcountry is incalculable, and though Methodism spread slowly, it early took hold in Britton's Neck and the Lower Lynches River areas. A Methodist church still in existence at this time 2017 is the Methodist church at Muddy Creek "Ebenezer" 1768 a record of a meeting at the church.

Other Methodist ministers became associated with Port's Ferry. Thomas Humphries, a Virginian who was one of the earliest missionaries to Georgia and who organized Little Pee Dee Circuit, married the Ports' daughter, Elizabeth, and located near the ferry where he became a wealthy rice planter. It was he who inducted James Jenkins into the Methodist Ministry. The Jenkins family lived near

Port's Ferry, where young Jenkins first went to school. His mother was the Revolutionary War heroine, "the Widow Jenkins," and his brothers fought with Marion. Seeing that Jenkins was serious in his call, Humphries took him on the round of his circuit, giving him counsel and instruction both privately and from the pulpit. In his memoirs Jenkins recounts an anecdote from the journey. "One night he (Humphries) called on me to pray; this was new work to me, but I made an attempt, and after blundering over a few words, thought I would close with the Lord's prayer, but was so frightened that I forgot that; he however, bore with my ignorance and encouraged me all he could." In his later years Jenkins instructed young ministers.

Francis Port died in 1811, leaving much of her very considerable estate, including the ferry, to her granddaughter, Mary Port (Humphries) Snow, wife of Samuel N. Snow. This couple migrated to Alabama, where they continued to promote and support the Methodist cause. Two other daughters of Elizabeth Port and Thomas Humphries married sons of the distinguished and beloved Methodist Bishop William Capers. Elizabeth married Samuel Wragg Capers, who was also a Methodist minister; and Ann Humphries married Gabriel Capers.

By 1820, former Governor David R. Williams, whose wife was the daughter of John Witherspoon of Witherspoon's Ferry, had succeeded in having the PeeDee River cleared for navigation from Georgetown to Society Hill. River traffic brought a period of prosperity to Port's Ferry. Only the redoubt, now a tangle of trees, and vines, and a few handsome tombstones, marks the location of the ferry. One of the tombstones tells a still different story: "Sacred to the memory of Mary Ann Davis, consort of H. Davis who was drowned January 11, 1849, preferring a watery grave to the devouring flames of steamship Richmond. Age 47 years 18 days."

In late 1781 and 1782, as the war drew to a close, loyalists in the Carolinas became increasingly desperate. In September 1781, North Carolina Loyalists Colonels Hector McNeil and David Fanning moved against the state capitol of Hillsborough, capturing 200 Continental soldiers, the governor, and leading Whigs. They released sixty Tory prisoners and escaped toward the coast. Throughout the winter, they stirred up local Loyalists along the Waccamaw and the Pee Dee and the Whig settlements. In the spring, the governor sent Francis Marion in a joint expedition against the Tories. After a brief skirmish, Ganey and Marion met at Burch's Mill in early June, and more than five hundred of Ganey's men laid down their arms. In July, Marion returned to the Santee.

David Fanning, a Tory, and his men, still in the area around Mars Bluff, were excluded from the deal. They attempted instead to make their way to the safety of British-occupied Charleston.

One of Marion's scouts along the Pee Dee was Andrew Hunter, a prosperous planter and mill owner in St. David's Perish. He owned several hundred acres of farmland near the junction of High Hill Creek and Black Creek (near the present boundary of Florence and Darlington counties), and his two grist mills had supplied meal and corn to the Whigs during the war.

Sometime in the late summer, Hunter unexpectedly came upon Fanning and his men. The Tories seized him and brought him to their camp on the Mars Bluff Ferry Road. After a perfunctory trial, Hunter was sentenced to hang after breakfast the next day. While the meal was being prepared, Hunter eluded his guards and jumped on Fanning's favorite horse. Named "Red Doe" (for her coloring, which resembled that of a deer), she was a rare animal, strong, fast, smart, and gentle. Hoping to save his prized mare, Fanning shouted to his men to shoot high at the fleeing prisoner. Hunter was wounded in the back, the bullet exiting just above the shoulder blade, but he kept riding down the Ferry Road, hoping to reach friends on the other side of the Great Pee Dee.

In the path to Hunter's escape were Middle Branch Creek and the canal for Gregg's Millpond, which cut across the road. Normally a bridge traversed the millpond canal, but as he approached, Hunter saw that the bridge was out. With the Tories pressing behind, he spurred on the mare to make the jump. She cleared the canal with a single, graceful bound.

Unable to make such a strenuous jump, Fanning's men were delayed in their pursuit. Hunter gained a lead, and when he reached the Great Pee Dee at Mars Bluff Ferry, the gallant mare plunged into the river and swam to the safety of the east side. Having made good his escape, Hunter paused on the bank, stood in his stirrups, and shouted defiantly to the Tories on the opposite shore, "Tell Captain Fanning the mare is mine, and he must catch Hunter before he can hang him!" Not only did Hunter have Fanning's horse, but his saddle, holsters, pistols, and papers. He sought shelter among friends in the Wahee Neck section of Prince Frederick Parish (modern Marion County) and was soon nursed back to health. Fanning and his men proceeded to Charleston.

Fanning prized this horse so much that he made several attempts to recover her. According to Fanning's account, sometime later he went to Hunter's home and seized his wife in hopes of exchanging her for the horse. Some authorities discount this version.

In September 1782, Fanning and a party of Tories returned to Mars Bluff in another attempt to recapture the horse, harassing local Whigs in the process. One of them, Robert Gregg, heard that Fanning was coming. As Fanning approached his home, Gregg tried to shoot him, but his gun failed. Gregg ran for nearby Polk Swamp to hide, but failed to make his escape before being shot in the hip by some of Fanning's men. Thinking that the wound was fatal, the Tories left him to die. He lived, but he was crippled for the rest of his life. According to local lore, Red doe was in the area, but had been moved to safety before Fanning's arrival. With only a handful of men with him, Fanning retreated to Charleston having failed again to find his horse.

In Charleston after the war's end, Fanning met Hunter riding Red Doe. The incensed Fanning challenged Hunter to a duel, but he failed to show at the appointed time. His last frustration came when a lawsuit to recover his horse was rejected by a Darlington court. Like several thousand other Loyalists, Fanning finally moved to Canada, where he died in 1825. Hunter kept Red Doe as long as she lived. When the prized horse died, the grateful Hunter buried her on a bluff on the Great Pee Dee River across which she had carried him to safety.

After the war, Hunter amassed eight plantations and many slaves. He represented St. David's Parish (1787–1788) and Darlington County (1796–1797) in the South Carolina House of Representatives and served on commissions for roads, navigations, and a new courthouse and jail. He died in Darlington District, South Carolina in 1823.

Red Doe Plantation

In the Mars Bluff area of present-day Florence County, about a mile and a half south of Francis Marion University, sits Red Doe, a grand old home nestled among old live oak trees. The home sits on the eastern side of Francis Marion Road, known in colonial times as the Georgetown and Cheraw Stagecoach Road.

Evander A. Gregg built the home that we know today as "Red Doe" in 1846. He was born on July 8, 1818, in the Mars Bluff area of Marion District and graduated from South Carolina College in 1837. His parents were Captain John Gregg and Jannet Gregg. The family worshipped in Hopewell Presbyterian Church, where Evander became a presiding elder. Around the time that Evander built this home, he married Sophronia E. Harris, daughter of Captain William Harris. After Sophronia's death in 1849, he married Elizabeth Crane, daughter of Sydney S. Crane of Columbia, South Carolina. A prosperous owner of several plantations and there enslaved laborers, Evander Gregg served in the Confederate States Army as Sergeant Major in Company C, Third South Carolina State Troops.

Shortly after the Civil War, in November 1865, the Greggs sold their Mars Bluff property to Simon Lucas (probably to dispose of the plantation of Evander's son by his first marriage, Henry Junius Gregg) and moved to Spartanburg. Born in 1846, Henry Junius Gregg served in Company I, Seventh South Carolina Cavalry. In April 1865, he died of wounds at a hospital in Farmville, Virginia. Evander and his family later moved to Arkansas and finally, to Marietta, Georgia, where he died in 1874. Simon Lucas, unable to pay off his loans, deeded the house back to Evander Gregg in January 1867. Afterwards, the property changed hands among Gregg descendants for more than a hundred years. Around 1834, the owner, J. W. Wallace, Jr., started calling the home "Red Doe" after hearing the story of Hunter's escape nearby.

The house is a one-story frame building with a full brick basement. While the basic plan was common throughout the eastern and southern United States in the early nineteenth century, the elevation of the main living rooms above the basement and the front "rain porch" with overhanging eaves both represent distinctive adaptations to the climate of the South Carolina Low country. The upper level was designed to catch any available breeze, while the basement included service areas and quarters for the household slaves. From 1940 to 1941, the house was extensively renovated by owners Marion Chisholm Wallace and Anne Pearce Wallace. In 1982, it was added to the National Register of Historic Places in recognition for its contribution to the country's architectural heritage. Today it is owned by the Pee Dee Rifles, Camp 1419 of the Sons of Confederate Veterans, who use the property for historic reenactments. They are working to stabilize the structure and intend for it to house their "War Between the States" and U.S. Military Museum.

By that time, the state government had been organized, with Marion in the Senate. He was no public speaker and avoided the limelight, but he graciously opposed the confiscation of the property of former enemies and refused to accept a general amnesty for any acts he had committed during the war, saying that he had done wrong to no man. Although the state sang his praises, it did little to reward him financially, nothing beyond a stipend as commander of Fort Johnson. Having served for three years without pay, Marion returned home to find Pond Bluff, his plantation, in ruins. With no more than a dozen slaves, he began to rebuild while continuing, as a moderate Federalist, to serve in the Senate and in other official capacities. He commanded a militia brigade until 1794.

A bachelor during the war, Marion married a cousin, Mary Esther Videau, on April 20, 1786, and her considerable estate allowed him to live comfortably. Within a few years, he owned about eighteen hundred acres and possessed upwards of seventy slaves. He and his bride were roughly the same age; they were in their fifties when they married, and the union produced no children. Loved and honored by his comrades-in-arms, Marion died on February 27, 1795. He was buried at Belle Isle Plantation in present-day Berkeley County, about ten miles west of St. Stephen. Mrs. Marion, who had a violent temper, very soon after her marriage, had so tamed this bold man.

Leonard Andrea

A decade after Marion's death, an itinerant biographer named Mason Weems produced a book called *The Life of General Francis Marion*, which became a national best seller. Francis Marion became an American hero, whose name was bestowed in honor on new towns and counties from South Carolina to Iowa. Lakes, forests, and colleges bore his name, and a generation of American boys grew up christened as "Marion" in the Pee Dee obscure Snow's Island retained a fame of its own as the fox's lair – hideaway of the great and glorious Swamp Fox.

Francis Marion was what I have termed to a super-patriot, enduring hardship and danger constantly from the fall of 1780, when he first met with the Williamsburg patriots until the evacuation of Charleston by the British. His area of operation was the eastern half of the South Carolina with occasional venture into North Carolina. More than 200 battles and skirmishes took place in South Carolina during the Revolution, Men of Marion's Brigade were involved in nearly one forth of them.

Sacred to the memory of Brig. Gen. Francis Marion, who departed this life on the twenty-seventh of February 1795 in the sixty- third year of his age; Deeply regretted by all his fellow citizens. History will record his worth, and rising generations embalm his memory, as one of the most distinguished patriots and heroes of the American Revolution, which elevated his native country to honor and independence, and secured to her the blessing of liberty and peace. This tribute of veneration and gratitude is erected in commemoration of the noble and disinterested virtue of the citizen; and the gallant exploits of the soldier; who lived without fear, and died without reproach.

Several years after the war of Revolution, all of Marion's men who claim for services are paid. A copy of each indent was made on the stub, and these stubs were bound into books. Named for the letters in the alphabet, the stubs and indents numbered. Most of the names on the lists were taken from the stubs of those old pay indents. This information can be found in South Carolina State Archives. (RHD)

William Willis Boddle died some years ago. In his lifetime, he compiled and had proof of 2,500 men who served with Marion. This was very valuable data for in the list he had hundreds of men whose records are not in the South Carolina Historical Commission.

I find that instead of being in strict order of the alphabet, the names ship around. After many names, of which I had knowledge, I took the liberty of adding "Also" when I knew the man had different spellings. All of them, when several, may have not used the spelling. This is helpful when attempting to find the wills or administrations on these men, in case several forms of spelling were used.

Colonels and Lieutenant-Colonels:

    Hugh Ervin
    John Ervin
    Hugh Giles
    Henry Hampton
    Richard Hampton
    Wade Hampton
    John Harden
    William Harden #1
    George Hicks
    Hugh Horry #2
    Peter Horry
    Edmund Hyrne

Joseph Kershaw
Abel Kolb
Henry Lee
Hezekiah Maham
Archibald McDonald
Stephen Miller
James Postell
Gabriel G. Powell
John Purvis
Richard Richardson
Thomas Screven
Maurice Simons
Charles H. Steward
William Clay Snipes
William Washington

Majors:

William Armstrong-uger#6
John Benson
Abram Buckholdt
William Butler
Samuel Cooper
James Conyers
George Ford
John Gamble
Derrill Hart
Charles Harden
Benjamin H John James
Robert Lide
Alexander McIntosh
Hugh McColl
Stephen Muller
Maurice Murphy
John Pearson

John Postell
Thomas Sabb
Keating Simons
Alexander Swinton
Tristam Thomas
Thomas Thompson
Alexander Windham
John Vanderhorst

Surgeons:

John Cleland
Henry C. Flagg
Oliver Hart
Matthew Irvine
William Reed
Alexander Rodgers
Perrin Theus
James Tourney

Captains:

Robert Allison
John Alston
William Alston
David Anderson
John Anderson
John Armstrong
Peter Bacot
John Barnwell
Thomas Ballard
John Blakeney
Samuel Boykin
Henry Britton

John Brown
Tarleton Brown
James Butler
John Butler
G. Sinkler Capers
Abraham Clayton
Clement Conyers
Daniel Conyers
George Cooper
Samuel Cooper
Robert Crawford
Joseph Dabbs
Aaron Daniel
Joseph Daniels
Amos Davis
Ransom Davis #7
Jeremiah Dixon
John Dozier
David DuBois-Ellerbe
Thomas Elliott
Charles Evans
Thomas Evans
James Ford
Samuel Foxworth
Phillip Frierson
John Futhey
Charles Gee
James Gee
Thomas Giles
William Gordon
John Graham
John T. Greene
James Gregg
Joseph Griffith
Stephen Guerry
Henry Hampton

John Hampton
John Hart
Edward Harden
Thomas Harvey
William Hendricks
William Hext
Daniel Horry
John Huggins
Mark Huggins
Edmund Irby
John Irvin
Stephen Jackson
Gavin James
John James, of the Lake
John James, of the High Hills
Jacob Jeannerette
Richard Johnson
Eli Kershaw
John Kimbrough
James Kincaid
George King
Francis Kinloch
Abram Lenud...also as leNud
Francis Lesesne
Thomas Lesesne
Thomas Lide
George Logan
Thomas Lynch Jr.
Guthridge Lyons
John McBride
James McCall
James Macauley...also McCauley
William McCleland
John McCord
William McCottry
George McCullough

Adam McDonald
James McDonald
Lawrence Manning
Edward Martin
Benjamin May
John Melton
Alexander McIntosh
Eleazor Mobley
Henry Mouzon...also as Henri
John Munnerlyn
William Murrell
Morrice Murphy
John Nelson
William Nettles
John Norwood
John Palmer
Thomas Parrot
Robert Pasley
Aaron Pearson
Moses Pearson
Claudius Pegues
John Perry
Edward Plowden
Thomas Potts
John Postell
Samuel Price
John Purvis...also as Pervis
Edward Richardson
William Richardson
Henry Rowe
Roger Sanders
John Singleton
Matthew Singleton
Arthur Simpkins
John Simons
John C. Smith...C for Carraway

William Spivey
William Snow
William Standard
John Starke
Robert Sutton
Samuel Taylor
James Theus
Robert Thomas
Tristram Thomas
Paul Trapier
Thomas Waites
Hugh Wardlaw
Thomas Williamson
Daniel Williams
Luke Whitefield
James Wilson
Richard Winn
William Withers
James Witherspoon
Gavin Witherspoon
John Witherspoon
Amos Windham
Peter Youngblood
Arnoldus Vanderhorst

Lieutenants:

Joseph Adair
John Adair
James Adair
William Adair
Jeremiah Allen
James H. Allison
James Anderson
Robert Armstrong

FRANCIS MARION

Samuel Bacot
Allard Belin
John Blakeney
William Bosquin
Daniel Britton
Henry Britton
Francis Boykin
Charles Brown
Benjamin Brown
John Bryan
Jacob Burnett
Samuel Burton
Robert Campbell
William Capers
Josiah Cantey
John Carrington
Thomas Chandler
James Coachman
Thomas Conn
Archibald Conner (Connor)
Isaac Conner
George Cooper
Daniel Cottingham
Arthur Cunningham
Aaron Daniel
John David
David Davis
Henry Davis
Charles DeWitt
Elias Dubose
Isaac Dubose
Robert Duke
Thomas Edwards
Thomas Elliott
James Ervin
Enoch Evans

George Evans
John Eubank
James Forgartie
Tobias Ford
Alexander Fraser
John Frierson
William Frierson
William Futhy
William Gamble
Wilson Glover
James Gordon
Roger Gordon
Zachariah Godbold
Joseph Graves
John Grayson
James Green
Samuel Guerry
James Hamilton
John Hamilton
Benjamin Harlow
Micajah Harriss
Charles Healty
John Hinds
Benjamin Hodge
Benjamin Huggins
William Huggins
Alexander Hume
John Jackson
Alexander James
James Jenkins
Reuben Jenkins
William Johnson
John Jones
Jonathan Jordan
John June
Thomas Kerwin

FRANCIS MARION

James Knight
Abraham Ladson
Andrew Lester
Charles Frederick Lesesne
Benjamin Lloyd
Edward Lloyd
Robert McAlpin
Daniel McCleary
James McDowell
Elisha McGee...also as Magee
James McKinney...also as McKinnie
Thomas McManness
William McMuldrough
John McMurray
Alexander McQueens
Duncan McRee...also as McRae
Gabriel Marion
John Martin
Jacob Michau
John Mikell
Charles Moody
James Munnerlyn
Isaac Neavel...also as Neville
Lewis Ogier
John Parker
Moses Pearson
John Perry
David Perkins
Daniel Pipkin
John Pledger
Joseph Pledger
Benjamin Postell
Hugh Postell
Thomas Potts, Jr.
Hugh Read
Joseph Read...also as Reid

Samuel Read...also as Reid
John Reed
John Reynolds
Richard Reynolds
Erasmus Rithmahler
John Rushing
Nathaniel Saunders
Joseph Scott
John Simons
Richard Singleton
James Smith
Samuel Smith
George Spivey
George Strother
John Sutton
James Terrell
Wright Wall
James Watts
John White
Jesse Wilds
John Wilkins
Ephriam Whittington
Shadrack Williamson
John Wilson
William Wilson
David Witherspoon
James Witherspoon
John Witherspoon
Robert Witherspoon

Comments by Andrea:
    You will note that some of the captains were later majors, etc. Among the privates you will note that many of these became officers.

    #1...This name is also as "Harding," as I have noted.

#2...Clerks sometimes spelled this name as it was and is now pronounced "O'ree." "Horry" was an early French family, and Horry County, S.C. is always pronounced "O'ree."

#3... This surname often spelled various ways, but really is "Maham."

#4... "Pervis" or "Perves" is also other spellings of "Purvis," as well as "Purves."

#5... "Buckholts" is now the way descendants spell this surname.

#6... Clerks often spelled this surname as it was and is now pronounced "U'gee" or "You'gee" and never as "Hu'ger."

#7... Ransom Davis always signed his name as "William Ransom Davis."

I had decided to place at foot of each page explanatory data, but I will not attempt it. It will make typing too much and hard. Many of these men, I have worked lines on and know the various ways the name was spelled.

Privates and noncommissioned officers:

John Abbott
Solomon Abbott
James Abernathy
John Abernathy
Alexander Adair
Benjamin Adair
Isaac Adair
James Adair
James Adair, Jr.
Drury Adams
George Adams
Godfrey Adams
John Adams
Joel Adams
Richard Adams
William Adams
John Adamson

William Adderson
Richard Addis
James Addington
Christopher Addison
Thomas Addison
William Addison
Bartlett Adkins
Shadrack Adkins...also known as Adkinson
William Aikins...also as Aiken
Levin Ainsworth
Archibald Akin
Ezekiel Akin
Alexander Alexander
Andrew Alexander
David Alexander
James Alexander
John Alexander
Matthew Alexander
Andrew Agnew
George Agnew...also as Egnew
James Allen
John Allen
Josiah Allen
Robert Allen
James Allison
Alexander Allison
Frances Alston
Joseph Alston
John Ammons
Thomas Ammons
David Anderson
Hugh Anderson
James Anderson
John Anderson
Stephen Anderson
Joseph Anderson

William Anderson
David Andrews
John Andrews
James Armstrong
John Armstrong
William Armstrong
James Arnett
John Arnett
Samuel Arnett
William Arnold
Anthony Ashby
George Ashford
John Askew...also as Eskew
Francis Austin
John Austin
Nathaniel Austin
Thomas Austin
Elijah Avent...now as Avant
William Axon
James Babcock
Samuel Bacot
John Baddeley
Ebenezer Bagnal...also as Bagnell
Isaac Bagnal
John Bagnal
Joseph Bailey
Moses Bailey
Moses Bayley II
Robert Baird
Alexander Baker
John Baker
Thomas Baker
Isaac Ball
Ambrose Ball
Richard Ball
John Ball

Jesse Ballard
Thomas Ballard
John Blake
William Banbury
Joshua Bar...also as Barr
Thomas Bar
William Barnes
Jesse Barnet...also as Barnett
John Barnet
Michael Barnet
Solomon Barnet
Nathan Barr
William Barr
James Barrentine...also as Barrington
Abraham Barron
Archibald Barron
Benjamin Barker
Edward Benbow
Arthur Bennett
Hugh Bennett
Matthew Bennett
Samuel Bennett
Andrew Benson
Benjamin Benson
William Benson
Lemuel Benton
William Berry
Jesse Beson...also as Beason
Goodman Bethea
Jesse Bethea
John Bethea
William Bethea
Robert Biggert
James Bigham
George Bird
William Bird

George Bishop
James Bishop
Nicholas Bishop
William Bishop
Elijah Blackburn
Bland Blackley
Alexander Black
Peter Black
Abram Blackwell..also as Abraham
Daniel Blackwell
Abram Blackwood
Charles Blackwood
John Ballard
John Blakeley
Edward Blake
John Blakeney
Robert Blakeney
Thomas Blakeney
Thomas Bland
William Bland
William Bentson
Michael Bates
William Blasinghame
Joseph Block
Thomas Block
William Block
James Bogan
Richard Bolton
Benjamin Bood
Jacob Barker
Robert Bartley
Thomas Barton
Andrew Baskin
Michael Bates
Israel Baxter
Joseph Booth

Enoch Booth
John Borland...also Bourland
John Bostick...also Bostwick
Matthew Bowman
Thomas Blakeney
Thomas Bland
Samuel Bland
Anthony Bonneau
Enoch Booth
George Booth
Joseph Booth
Matthew Booth
John Bourland
John Bostic
Benjamin Bowers
William Bowler...also Bouler
Matthew Bowman
John Bowler
Thomas Bowter also Boiter
William Bozewood...also Boswood
Evan Boyd
John Boyd
William Boyd
Barnwell Boykin
Samuel Boykin
Aaron Boynton
John Bozeman...also Boazman
John Bradford
Robert Bradford
Arthur Bradley
James Bradley
Roger Bradley
Samuel Bradley
John Bannon
Roger Bratton
William Bratton

Joshua Braveboy
Abraham Bretar
John Brewer
David Brinton
John Brinton
Adam Brisbane
Daniel Britton
Francis Britton
James Bridges
Richard Brockington
Joseph Brooker
Charles Brooks
John Bood
Michael Bood...also Boud
Anthony Bonneau
Capers Boone
Frederick Boone
Thomas Boone
Micajah Brooks
Alpheus Brown
Dennis Brown
Elijah Brown
James Brown
John Brown
Tarleton Brown
William Brown
Charles Browne
Charles Brunson
Daniel Brunson...once Brownson
James Brunson
Josiah Brunson...also Bronson
William Brunson
Joseph Bryan
Lewis Bryan
Simon Bryan
William Bryan

Gray Bryant
Richard Bryant
Hardy Bryant
William Bryant
Barnard Budener
David Buche
John Bouche
Joseph Bulkley…also Buckley
John Burbridge…also Burbage
Daniel Bullock
John Burgess
Joel Burgess
Joseph Burgess
William Burgess
Ephriam Burkett
John Burkett
Levi Burkett
Samuel Burkett
Benjamin Burnett
John Burns
Robert Burns
Robert Burton
Samuel Burrows…also Burroughs
William Burrows
William W. Burrows
Joseph Burton
John Butler
James Butler
Thomas Butler
William Butler
Jacob Buxton #1
Samuel Buxton
William Byers
John Byrd-Sutton Byrd

#1...Noted a Jacob Buxton as a captain in Orangeburg under Col. Wm. Henderson of Gen. Thomas Sumter's Brigade... Andrea

    Drury Cade
    John Cade
    Robert Cade
    Stephen Cade
    William Cade
    Abner Cain
    John Cain
    James Caldwell
    Joseph Caldwell
    Samuel Caldwell
    William Caldwell
    Daniel Callahan
    John Callum
    John Cameron
    Josiah Cameron
    Duncan Campbell
    George Campbell
    James Campbell
    John Campbell
    Michael Campbell
    Robert Campbell
    Samuel Campbell
    Thomas Campbell
    James Cantey
    John Cantey
    Phillip Cantey
    Josiah Cantey
    William Cantey
    Zachariah Cantey
    Charles Cantley
    Daniel Cannon
    George Cannon
    Ephriam Cannon

David Cannon
Henry Cannon
William Capers
John Capps
Adam Carican...also Carrigan
Alexander Carnes
Christian Carr
Edmund Carr
William Carraway
John Carroll
Thomas Carsan...also Carson
Walter Carsan
James Carter
John Carter
Matthew Carter
Robert Carter
John Casey
John Caskey
Benjamin Cassels
John Cassels
Jesse Cassity
Zachariah Cassity
Henry Cato
Richard Champ
James Chambers
Abednego Chandler
George Chandler
Isaac Chandler
Jacob Chandler
Jesse Chandler
Joel Chandler
William Chandler
Robert Chapan...also Chapin
Lawrence Charles
George Cheney...also Chaney
William Cheney

John Chemey
George Cherry
Jacob Cherry
William Cherry
John Chestnut
John China of Sumter County
John Chisholm
Alexander Chisholm
Michael Church
David Clanton
Anthony Clark
James Clark
John Clark
Joseph Clark
Thomas Clark
Lawrence Clayton
Joseph Clements
Josiah Clements
Charles Clinton
James Coachman
Robert Coachman
Marmaduke Coate
Thomas Cochran
James Cockfield
Hugh Coffee
John Coffin
Benjamin Coker
Nathan Coker
Thomas Coker
David Cole
James Cole
John Cole
Richard Cole
Alexander Colcolough
Abner Coleman
Charles Coleman

Francis Coleman
Jacob Coleman
John Coleman
William Coleman
Benjamin Collar
Edmund Collins
Daniel Collins
Gary Collins
Jonah Collins
Lewis Collins
John Collier
Samuel Commander
Thomas Commander
George Con...also Conn
Thomas Conn
Matthew Cone
Thomas Connor
Adam Connor
Archibald Connor
Isaac Connor
James Connor
Elimeach Cook
West Cook
William Cook
James Cooke
John Cooke
Reuben Cooke
George Cooper
Sylvanus Cooper
William Cooper
William J. Cooper
Charles Conyers
James Conyers
John Conyers
 Stran Conyers...really Straughn
 Thomas Corbitt...also Corbett

Samuel Cordes
John Cork
Thomas Cotton
Samuel Cotton
Dill Cottingham
William Council
John Cousar
Robert Courtney
Stephen Courtney
John Covington
William Coward
Robert Cowley...also Cooly
Allen Cox
Emanuel Cox
Christopher Cox
James Cox
John Cox
Josiah Cox
Manuel Cox...also Emanuel
Samuel Cox
William Cox
James Craig
Alexander Crawford
Robert Crawford
William Crawford
Samuel Crews
Robert Crockat...also Crockett
Samuel Crockat
Richard Creech
Stephen Creech
William Creech
Charles Creighton
James Crocker
Abraham Croft
William Cropps...also Krepps
Thomas Crosby

John Cross
Samuel Cross
Edward Crossland
Gilbert Croswell
William Crow
Alexander Cunningham
Arthur Cunningham
George Cunningham
James Cunningham
John Cunningham
Patrick Cunningham
Charles Curry
Jacob Curry
Peter Curry
Stafford Curry
Adam Cusak...also Cusack
Jacob Dabbs
Joseph Dabbs
Aaron Daniel
James Daniel
John Daniel
Thomas Daniel
Richard Daniel
Ezekiel Daniel...also Zekiel
Henry Danseller...now Dantzler
Asa Darby
John Darlington
Josiah David
Arthur Davis
Benjamin Davis
Henry Davis
Isham Davis
John Davis
James Davis
Thomas Davis
Francis Davenport

Joshua Dinkins
John Dobbin
Hugh Dodds
William Dawkins
Britton Dawson
William Dawson
Henry Day
John Day
Joseph Day
Peter Day
William Day
Robert Dearington
John Deas
Andrew deHay
John deHay...also DeHay
Hardy deLoach...also DeLoach
John deLoach
Michael deLoach
Samuel deLoach
William deLoach
John Denning
Isaiah Dennis
Richard Dennis
James Denton
Lewis Devant
Stephen DeVeau (deVeau)
John DeWeen...also Deween
Harris DeWitt
Reuben DeWitt
William DeWitt
Garret Dial
John Dial
Jeremiah Dial
John Dick
Joseph Dick
Robert Dick

Thomas Dick
William Dick
David Dickey...also Dickie
Edward Dickey
George Dickey
John Dickey
Robert Dickey
Stuart Dickey
Hugh Dickson
James Dickson
John Dickson
Joel Dickson
Michael Dickson
Matthew Dickson
William Dickson
Nicholas Dillard
Joshua Dillon
Robert Dingle
Patrick Dollard
Peter Doney
William Dortch
William Doughty...also Doty
Alexander Douglas
James Douglas
Jesse Douglas
John Douglass...also Douglas
Joshua Douglas
Sherrod Douglas
Solomon Douglas
William Doughtry
Alexander Dove
Benjamin Dove
John Doyal...also Doyle
John Downing
William Drake
Julius Driggers

Alexander Drumm
Andrew DuBose
Daniel DuBose
Elias DuBose
Isaac DuBose
Joseph DuBose
John DuBose
Peter Dubose
Samuel DuBose
William DuBose
Jesse Duesto...also DuEsto
Thomas Dudley
Edmund Duke
Joseph Duke
Robert Duke
Benjamin Dukes
James Duncan
John Duncan
John Dunlap...also Dunlop
Robert Dunlap
Samuel Dunlap
William Dunlap
James Duling
John Duling
James Dunn
John Dunman
William Dunn
Levi Durand
Henry DuRant
Thomas DuRant
Michael DuVal
Nathaniel Dwight
John Dye...also Die
James Dysell
Daniel Eaddy
Henry Eaddy

Samuel Edwards
Henry Eddy
Henry Easterling
David Eddingfield
John Finly
Charles Finklea
Reading Fields
James Fisher
Charles Fledger
Alexander Fleming
James Fleming II
William Eddingfield
John Elam
William Ellerbe
Thomas Ellerbe
Richard Elliss…also Eliss
Robert Ellison
Theophilus Elsworth
Joshua Emanuel
John English
Joshua English
James Ervin
John Ervin
Samuel Ervin
Henry Etheridge
Samuel Etheridge
Benjamin Evans
Burwell Evans
Charles Evans
Enoch Evans
Ezer Evans
George Evans
Isaac Evans
James Evans
John Evans
Josiah Evans

Nathan Evans
Nathaniel Evans
Richard Evans
Samuel Evans
William Evans
Samuel Ewing
William Fair
Zachariah Farmer...also Zach
Thomas Farrar
John Faulkner
Moses Ferguson
James Ferguson
John Ferguson
Thomas Ferguson
William Ferguson
Stephen Ferrell
James Fitzpatrick
Christopher Fitzsimmons
Paul Finley
John Finley
Uzza Finley
James Finly
John Finly
Charles Finklea
Reading Fields
James Fisher
Charles Fledger
Alexander Fleming
James Fleming II
James Fleming I
John Fleming
Robert Fleming
William Fleming
William Fletcher
Henry Flowers
John Flowers

Joshua Flowers
Archibald Flowers
Albert Ford
George Ford
Henry Ford
John Ford
Malachi Ford
Robert Ford
Thomas Ford
Stephen Ford
Patrick Forbes
Thomas Foreman
Isaac Foreman
Arthur Fort
Moses Fort
Owen Fort
Andrew Fraser...also Frazier
James Fraser
William Fraser
Henry Foster
John Foster
Moses Foster
William Fountain
James Fowler
John Fowler
Richard Fowler
William Fowler
William Fox
James Foxworth
Samuel Foxworth
Absalon Frierson
George Frierson
James Frierson
John Frierson
Joshua Frierson
Phillip Frierson

Robert Frierson
William Frierson
William Frierson, Jr.
Benjamin Fuller
John Fuller
Whitmarsh Fuller
James Fullerton
Robert Futhy
John Fulton
Thomas Fulton
Willliam Fullwood
John Gainey
William Gainey
Peter Galloway
Hugh Gamble...also Gambel
James Gamble
John Gamble
Stephen Gamble
Robert Gamble
Samuel Gamble
William Gambrell
Joshua Gardner
John Gardner
William Gardner
William Garland
Samuel Garner
Joseph Garnett
Ephriam Gaskins
Thomas Gasque...also Gasquet
James Gaston
Jesse George
John George
Richard George
William George
Michael Gibbons
Gideon Gibson

Gilbert Gibson
Guyon Gibson
Isaac Gibson
Jacob Gibson
James Gibson
John Gibson
Joseph Gibson
Luke Gibson
Phineas Gibson
Robert Gibson
Thomas Gibson
William Gibson
Abraham Giles
Robert Giles
Thomas Giles
Andrew Gillispie
James Gillespie
Samuel Gillespie
Edward Gilmore
James Gilmore
Joshua Glass
William Glenn
Benjamin Godfrey
John Godfrey…also Godfry
James Godbold
Zachariah Godbold
Arthur Goodson
James Goodson
Jonathan Goodson
William Goodson
Harris Goodwin
Richard Goodwin
Francis Goodwyn
Lewis Goodwyn
William Goodwyn
Brittan Goodwyn

David Goodwyn
Alexander Gordon
George Gordon
James Gordon
John Gordon
Moses Gordon
Thomas Gordon
Francis Gordon
William Gordon
James Graham
William Graham
James Grant
William Grant
John Gray
Solomon Gray
Daniel Gregg
David Gregg
James Gregg
John Gregg
Isaac Gregory
Robert Gregory
Daniel Green
Richard Green
Lewis Graves
William Gray
Benjamin Green
William Green
Benjamin Griffin
David Griffin
John Griffith
Morgan Griffith
James Grimes
William Grissom
Nathaniel Guyton
William Gwinn
Isaac Haddock

Davis Hagens
John Haig
Henry Haynesworth…also Hainsworth
Joseph Haynesworth
James Hair
Silas Hales
James Hall
Matthew Hall
James Hamilton
John Hammett
James Hanna
John Hanna
Robert Hanna
William Hanna
James Hannah
Richard Hannah
William Hannah
Edward Harden
Benjamin Harper
Matthew Harper
Samuel Harper
Solomon Harper
William Harper
John Harrell
Lewis Harrell
Levi Harrell
Benjamin Harrelson
William Harrelson
John Harrington
Reuben Harris
Henry Harrison
Josiah Harrison
Arthur Hart
Phillip Hart
William Hart
Richard Harvin

Isaac Hawkins
James Hawkins
David Hay
George Hayes
Jesse Hayes
Matthew Hayes
William Hayes
Richard Hazelton
William Hazelton
William Hazelton II
Thomas Heagins
William Heathley
William Heathley, Jr.
Jesse Heathly
Robert Heathly
Alexander Henderson
Archibald Henderson
James Henderson
Wilson Henderson
John Herndon
Robert Heriot
William Heriot
James Huestis
John Huestis
Matthew Huestis
William Huestis
James Hewsties
Thomas Hext
Arthur Hicklin
Benjamin Hicks
George Hicks
John Hicks
Robert Hicks
John Hickson
Edward Hindley
Samuel Hines

Patrick Hinds
Clayburn Hinson...also Henson
William Hinson
John Hixon
Benjamin Hodge
Jonathan Hodge
James Hodge
Benjamin Hodges
Elias Hodges
Henry Hodges
Henry Hodge
Isham Hodges...also Isom
John Hodges
Joseph Hodges
Robert Hodges
Welcome Hodges
John Hogan
Benjamin Holladay
Daniel Holladay...also Holliday
William Holleman
Richard Holley...also Holly
James Holloway
Elias Hollingsworth
David Hopkins
Daniel Horry
Archibald Hood
Allen Hood
John Hood
Henry Horton
Edward Hoole
Enoch Hoover...also Huber
Benjamin Howard
Edward Howard
John Howard
Arthur Howell
Thomas House

Isom House...also Isham
Thomas Huckaby...also Hucabee
Samuel Huckaby...also Huckabee
Noah Hubbard
William Huddleston
Joseph Hudson
William Hudson
Samuel Hughes
John Hughs
John Huggins
Mark Huggins
William Huggins
Anthony Hughes
John Hume
Charles Humphries
Creswell Hunt
James Hunt
Andrew Hunter
Elisha Hunter
John Hutson
Henry Hyrne
Abram Ingram
Alexander Ingram
Arthur Ingram
Charles Irby
John Irvin
Arthur Jackson
Benjamin Jackson
Charles Jackson
David Jackson
John Jackson
Stephen Jackson
William Jackson
Alexander James
Gavin James
George James

James James
Robert James
William James
William D. James
William Jameson
Nicholas Jasper
Elias Jaudon
James Jaudon
Peter Jaudon
Nathaniel Jefferies
Thomas Jefferies
Thomas Jeffreys
Charles Jenkins
John Jenkins
James Jenkins
Reuben Jenkins
Edward German
Azel John
Jesse John
Thomas John
David Johnson
Gilbert Johnson
James Johnson
John Johnson
Benjamin Jolly
James Jolly
Wilson Jolly
James Jones
Thomas Jones
William Jones
John Jordan
Moses Jordan
Robert Jordan
Thomas Jordan
William Jordan
Henry Joyce

William Joyce
Ezekiel Joyner
Joseph Joyner
John Joyner
Solomon June
John Justice
Simon Justice
Thomas Kanaday...also Cannady
John Karr
Thomas Karwan...also Kirwen
Isaac Keels
James Keels
John Keels
John Kean
John Keely
Matthew Keely
Robert Keely
Thomas Keely
William Keil
Cornelius Keith
James Kelly
Joseph Kelly
John Kelly
Peter Kelly
Alexander Kennedy
Joseph Kennedy
John Kennedy
David Kennedy
Stephen Kennedy
Thomas Kennedy
William Kennedy
Adam Kerrick
Henry Kerrick
Archibald Knox
James Knox
Robert Knox

Joseph Kershaw
Henry Kilgore
Frederick Kimball...also Fred
John Kimbrough
James Kincaid
John Kincaid
James Kirby
John Kirkland
Reuben Kirkland
Richard Kirkland
William Kirkland
Niglet Knight
Thomas Knight
Benjamin Koker...also Coker
Benjamin Kolb
Jehu Kolb
Peter Kolb
Thomas Kolb
Thomas LaBruce...also La Bruce
Thomas Ladson
John Lake
John Lambert
Henry Lancaster
Samuel Landrum
Drury Lane
David Large
John Larrimore
William Latta
William Law
Andrew Lee
John Lee
Robert Lee
Stephen Lee
Thomas Lee
Jeremiah Legett...also LeGette
Peter Lequex

Samuel LeQuex
James Leister
Thomas LeNoir...also Lenoir
Henry Lenud...also LeNud
William Leslie
John Lesly
Andrew Lester
Henry Lewis
William Lewis
Moses Liddel
Thomas Lide
William Lide
William Lifrage...also LiFrage
James Liles
John Lindsay
Robert Lindsay
Alexander Logan
Anthony Logan
Andrew Logan
David Logan
Henry Logan
Francis Logan
John Logan
John Logan, Jr.
William Logan
John Lessley
Samuel Logue
James Long
Levy Long
Thomas Long
Andrew Love
Drury Love
John Love
Christopher Lowry
John Lowry
Matthew Lowry

Richard Lowry
Robert Lowry
William Lowry
George Lowther
Zilpha Lowther
Owen Luke
Edward Lowther
Isaac Lowe
John Lummos
Drewry Lundy
John Lundy
John Lyon
William Lyon
Matthias Lewis
Josiah Lewis
Joseph Lewis II
Robert Lewis
Thomas Lewis
William Lewis
David Macauley
John Magill
Hezekiah Maham
John Makie
James Mann
James Manning
Moses Manning
William Manson
John Marcus
James Marlo
John Marion
Joseph Marion
Robert Marion
Abraham Markley...also Markly
John T. Marsh
John Marshall
Robert Marshall

Beasley Marmon
David Martin
Edmund Martin
Jeremiah Martin
James Martin
John Martin
Joseph Martin
Richard Martin
Robert Martin
Roger Martin
William Martin of the Cheraws
Moses Martin
Matthew Martin
Charles Mason
William Mason
James Massey
James Mathis
John Mathis
William Mathis
Benjamin Matthews
David Matthews
Isaac Matthews
John Matthews
Joseph Matthews
Samuel Matthews
William Matthews
Edward Maxwell
James Maxwell
Samuel Maxwell
Andrew Mays
James Mayes
Samuel Mayes
Robert Mayfield
Thomas Meadows
William Mellet
Daniel Michau

William Michau
Solomon Mickles
John Mikell
John Mikell, Jr.
John Mims
John Miles
Richard Miles
William Miles
Alexander Miller
Andrew Miller
Matthew Miller
James Miller
John Miller
Phillip Miller
Nathiniel Miller
Robert Miller
William Miller
Gilbert Mills
Jesse Mills
Thomas Mills
Jesse Minton
Benjamin Mitchell
John Mitchell
Nimrod Mitchell
Thomas Mitchell
Thomas Mitchum
Maraday Mixon
Michael Mixon
Francis Mixon
John Mixon
Samuel Mixon
Benjamin Moberly
Clement Moberly
Edward Moberly, Sr.
Edward Moberly, Jr.
Eleazer Moberly

John Moberly
William Moberly
John Moffit
John Montfort
George Montgomery
Henry Montgomery
Hugh Montgomery
James Montgomery
John Montgomery
Nathaniel Montgomery
Robert Montgomery
Samuel Montgomery
Addrew Moodie...also Mootie Moody
Andrew Moody
Roderick Moody
Gully Moore
Jeremiah Moore
James Moore
John Moore
John Moore, Jr.
Levi Moore
Lewis Moore
William Moore
John Moon
Samuel Morgan
John Morrell...also Morrall
James Mikell
Benjamin Morris
George Morris
John Morris
Thomas Morris
Daniel Morrison
Joseph Morrison
John Morrow
Joseph Morrow
Samuel Morrow

Thomas Morrow
Andrew Muckldrough
David Muckldrough
Hugh Muckldrough
James Muckldrough
John Muckldrough
John Munnerlyn
Malachi Murfee...also Murphee
Moses Murfee
Alexander Murray
John Murray
William Murray
Edward Murphy
James Murphy
William Murrell
John McAdam
Alexander McAlpine
George McBay
Vardry McBee
Andrew McBride
Hugh McBride
James McBride
William McBride
Alexander McCain
Peter McCain
Alexander McCalpin
Robert McCalpin
Solomon McCalpin
John McCamey
James McCamon
John McCammon
George McCall
Henry L. McCall
Hugh McCall
James McCall
Nathaniel McCallister

David McCance...also McCants
William McCance
Patrick McCann
Charles McCants
David McCants
John McCants
Joseph McCants
Robert McCants
Thomas McCants
William McCants
William McCarley
Moses McCarley
Jeremiah McCarter
James McCarter
John McCarter
Moses McCarter
William McCarter
John McCaw
Samuel McCaskill...also McKaskill
James McCauley
John McCauley
William McClain
Daniel McClane
Hugh McClane
John McClary
John McCleary
Dennis McClaskey
James McClelland
Samuel McClelland
Robert McClelland
William McClelland
Finney McClenehan
Samuel McClinton...also McLinton
David McClosky
Joseph McClosky
William McClosky

Daniel McClure...also McLure
Hugh McClure
James McClure
John McClure
Daniel McCollom
George McConnell
Hugh McConnell
James McConnell
John McConnell
Thomas McConnell
Reuben McConnell
Adam McCool
John McCool
Joseph McCool
David McCord
John McCord
Hugh McCormick
Alexander McCowen
Alexander McCown
James McCown
John McCown
Moses McCown
Samuel McCown
David McCoy...also McCay
Edward McCoy...also McKoy
Elijah McCoy
Daniel McCoy
James McCoy
John McCoy
Stephen McCoy
James McCracken
John McCrea...also McRae
Joseph McCrea
Thomas McCrea
Robert McCrea
James McCreight

Duncan McCreevan
Robert McCreight
Andrew McCullough...also McCullock
Hugh McCullough
James McCullough
John McCullough
John J. McCullough
Robert McCullough
Samuel McCullough
Thomas McCullough
William McCullough
James McCutcheon...also McKutcheon
John McCutcheon
Patrick McCutcheon
Edward McDaniel
James McDaniel
John McDavid
John McDill
Archibald McDonald
Charles McDonald
Francis McDonald
Henry McDonald
James McDonald
John McDonald
Martin McDonald
William McDonald
John McDow
Andrew McDowell
David McDowell
John McDowell
Samuel McDowell
William McDowell
Adam McElduff
Adam McElveen
James McElwee...also McIlwee
Samuel McElvin

Andrew McIlvin
Henry Muckelween...also McElveen
James McIlvaine...also McElvaine
John McIlvany
Robert McIlvain
William McInvennay
William McElveen
Edward McFadden
Patrick McFadden
Isaac McPhadden...also McFadden
Robert McFadden
Thomas McFadden
Thomas McFadden
William McFadden
John McFarlin
McFarling II
Edward McFarlane
Archibald McFarren
Andrew McFarren
James McFarren
James McGarrity
John McGaw
William McGaw
Elisha McGee...also Magee
James McGee
Patrick McGee
Thomas McGee
William McGee
John McGill
Samuel McGill
Charles McGinney
James McGowan
John McGowen
Solomon McGraw
Peter McGraw
Thomas McGuinness

Alexander McGuire
James McIlwee
Alexander McIntosh
John McIntosh
Lachlan McIntosh
Luther McIntosh...also Lowther
William McIntosh
Daniel McIntire...also McIntyre
Evander McIver...also Avender
James McKay
Adam McKee
John McKee
Joseph McKee
Robert McKee
Thomas McKee
Hugh McKelvy
John McKelvy
John McKemmy
William McKeene
Samuel McKenney...also McKinney
Joseph McKenzie
William McKenzie
Archibald McKewen
William McKinny
James McKnight
John McKnight
Moses McKnight
Thomas McKnight
John McKnit
Andrew McLean
Stephen McLeland
John McLendon...also McClendon
James McMaster
John McMaster
Patrick McMaster
William McMaster

John McMahan
William McMahan
William McMichael
Daniel McMillan
Robert McMillen
Andrew McMuldrough...also McMuldrow
Hugh McMuldrough
James McMuldrough
William McMuldrough
Henry McMurdy
Samuel McMurray
Thomas McMurray
James McNabb
William McNabb
Joel McNatt
James McNeil...also McNell
James McNeer...also McNair
James McPherson
Isaac McPherson
Alexander McQueen
James McTier...also McTyer
Mackey McNatt
Isaac Neavel...also Neville
David Neely
George Neely
George Neely
Hugh Neely
Samuel Neely
James Neilson...not for Nelson
William Neilson
David Nelson
Isaac Nelson
Robert Nelson
Samuel Nelson
Thomas Nelson
William Nelson

George Nettles
Isham Nettles
Jesse Nettles
Joseph Nettles
Robert Nettles
William Nettles
Zachariah Nettles
John NeSmith
Lemuel Nesmith...also Nasmith
Robert Nesmith
Samuel Nesmith
Thomas Nesmith
Thomas Newman
James Nickells
Thomas Nickells...also Nickles
Stephen Nixon
James Nobles...also Noble
Nicholas Nobles...also Nick
William Noland...also Nolan
John Norris
Patrick Norris
Robert Norris
Thomas Norris
William Northant
Hugh Norton
James Norton
John Norwood
Thomas Norwood
Samuel Norwood, Jr.
Thomas Nugent
Joseph Nunn
Dennis O'Brian
George O'Brian
Jesse O'Brian
William O'Brian
Abraham Odem...also Odum

Benjamin Odem...also O'Dom
Daniel Odem...also Odom
Fluke Odem
Hezekiah Odem
Ezekiel Oglilvie...also Ogilvie
John Ogilvie
Alexander Oliver
James Oliver
John Oliver
Peter Oliver
William Oliver
John O'Neal
William Orr
Lewis Owen
Benjamin Owens
James Owens
Peter Owens
Samuel Owens
Thomas Owens
Zachariah Owens
Benjamin Outlaw
Daniel Pack
John Pack
Luke Pack
Matthew Page
John Paisley
Robert Paisley
Peter Palmer
Thomas Palmer
John Pamor
Moses Parker
William Parler
James Parnell
William Parnell
Thomas Parrot
James Parsons

William Parsons
Andrew Patterson
John Patterson
Robert Patterson
Jacob Patton
Matthew Patton
Matthew Paul
William Paul
Anthony Pawley
Percival Pawley
Aaron Pearson
Phillip Pearson
Alexander Peden...also Paden
David Peden
Claudius Pegues...also PeGuies
William Pegues
Abraham Pearce
Thomas Penny
Nathan Peoples...also Peebles
John Perdrieu
David Perkins
Isaac Perkins
Lewis Perkins
James Perkins
William Perkins
Edward Perry
James Perry
Job Perry
Lewis Perry
Samuel Perry
Enoch Pearson
John Peterkin
Robert Petticrue
Abraham Phelps
John Phillips
Edward Pierson

John Pierce
John Piggot
John Piggot, Jr.
Nathaniel Piggot
Micajah Pickett
John Pitts
Roger Player
Robert Player
William Player
John Pledger
Philip Pledger
William Plowden
Luke Poke...likely Polk
John Poke
Daniel Poke
Barnaby Pope
John Pope
Benjamin Port
Francis Port
Benjamin Porter
John Porter
John Poston
Joseph Poston
Thomas Poston
John Postell
Thomas Potts
Thomas Potts II
Jesse Potts
John Potts
Roger Potts
Andrew Postell
John Powell I
John Powell II
Thomas Powe...also Poe
Nicholas Powers
Anthony Pouncey

Jonathan Presswood
Thomas Presswood
Aaron Prescott
James Prevatt
William Price
Roger Pouncey
Evan Pugh...also Pou
Alexander Purvis
Gilbert Purvis
William Purvis
John Pyatt
John Raburn...also Rabon
John Ragin
Michael Rasher
John Raspberry
John Rawlinson...also Rollinson
Alexander Ray
John Rayfield...also Rafield
Murray Reed
Matthew Reed
Ephriam Roose...likely Reese
Lazarus Reeves
Jesse Register
Joshua Register
Joseph Reid
George Reid
Isaac Rembert
Joseph Reynolds
James Rice
Henry Richborough...also Henri
James Richborough
John Richborough...now Richburg
William Richbourg
John Ricks...also Rix
Richard Ridgill
William Ridgill

Patrick Riley
John Ritchie...also Ritchey
Frederick Rivers
Thomas Roach
William Roan
Amos Roberts
John Roberts I
John Roberts II
Lewis Roberts
Roger Roberts
Stephen Roberts
Peter Robert...also Pierre Robert
Andrew Roe
Solomon Roe
Walter Roe
Edward Rogers
Nathaniel Rodgers
William Rodgers
Andrew Rogers
David Rogers
James Robertson
John Rochelle
George Rollinson...also Rawlinson
Richard Rollinson
William Rollinson
John Rose
Francis Ross
James Ross
Roberts Ross...perhaps Robert
Moses Ross
William Ross
Neil Rouse...also Neal
Edward Rowell
Jonathan Rowell
Valentine Rowell
James Rowlaine

Job Rowley
George Ruff...not Roof
Richard Russell
Stephen Russell
Morgan Sabb
Thomas Sabb
George Sadler
David Sadler
Richard Sadler
Peter Salter
Job Saltzer
Daniel Sansbury
John Satterwhite
Andrew Sauders
George Saunders
Isaac Saunders
William Saunders
Nathan Savage
Richard Savage
Samuel Savage
Achilles Sax
Yancey Saxon
John Sawyer
Hardy Sellers
Howell Sellers
John Sellers
William Sellers
Edward Sexton
Alexander Scott
Archibald Scott
Cason Scott
John Scott
Samuel Scott
Thomas Scott
William Scott
Elisha Screven

William Screven
Thomas Scurry
Samuel Shoemaker
Jesse Simmons
Jeremiah Simmons
Cleburn Simms
Samuel Simms
Thomas Simms
William Simms
David Simons
Charles Simons
James Simons
Maurice Simons
Peter Simons
Samuel Simons
Shadrack Simons
William Simpson
Benjamin Singleton
John Singleton
Richard Singleton
William Singleton
Peter Sinkler
Charles Sly...also Sligh
John Smiley...also Smyley
Charles Smith
Daniel Smith
George Smith
Jeremiah Smith
James Smith
John Smith
Richard Smith
Samuel Smith
Stephen Smith
Thomas Smith
Thomas Spraggins
Thomas Spratt

Shadrack Stanley
William Stackhouse
John Staggers
Thomas Stafford
John Staley
Peter Staley
John Starke
Thomas Starke
William Starke...also Stark
Edward Stedman
Aaron Steele...also Steel
Alexander Steele
Charles Steele
Isaac Steele
John Stephens
Adam Stewart
Hugh Stewart
James Stewart
John Stewart
Thomas Stewart
William Stewart
Thomas Stokes
John Tamplet
Benjamin Tanner
Alexander Tete...and as Tait
Richard Tate
Samuel Tate
Francis Taylor
George Taylor
John Taylor
Jonathan Taylor
Oliver Taylor
Samuel Taylor
Edward Teal
Amos Thames...also Themes
Daniel Thomas

Edward Thomas
Josiah Thomas
Samuel Thomas
Tristam Thomas
William Thomas
Nathan Thompson
Eleazer Thorp
Abner Timmons
Jesse Timmons
John Timmons
Samuel Timmons
Thomas Timmons
James Tisdale...also Teasdale
John Tisdale...also Tisdell
John Tison...also Tyson
Haywood Todd
John Todd
Richard Todd
Arthur Tomlinson
John Tomlinson
Nathaniel Tomlinson
William Tomlinson
Obed Tootles
Henry Townsend
James Townsend
John Townsend
Light Townsend
Thomas Townsend
John Travis
George Tubb
Amos Tubbs
Daniel Tucker
David Tucker
James Tucker
Robert Tucker
Joseph Turnbull

George Turner
Josiah Turner
James Turner
John Tyler
Samuel Tyler
John Valentine
William Vance
Edward Vann
Jesse Vann
Robert Vardell
Jeremiah Vereen...also Vareen
William Vereen
Benjamin Vaughan
Christopher Vaughn
David Vaughn
James Venable
John Venable
Jacob Vickers
Jesse Vining
Abel Waddell
Thomas Wade
William Wadington
John Waid
Joseph Waddell
Michael Waldrop
Adam Walker
Alexander Walker
Charles Walker
James Walker
John Walker, Sr.
John Walker, Jr.
Phillip Walker
Samuel Walker
Tandy Walker
Thomas Walker
William Walker

John Walkup I
John Walkup II
John Walkup III
Samuel Walkup
James Wallace...also Wallis
John Wallace
Joseph Wallace
Oliver Wallace
Peter Wallace
Robert Wallace
Thomas Wallace
William Wallace
Daniel Walsh
Elias Ward
John Ward
Joshua Ward
Nathan Ward
Thomas Ward
John Wardlaw
Joseph Wardlaw
William Wardlaw
David Warner
Abraham Warnook
George Warren
James Warren
Joseph Warren
Robert Warren
Samuel Warren
Charles Waters
Philemon Waters
Rawley Waters...also Rolly and Raleigh
West Waters
Samuel Watkins
William Watt
Andrew Watts
George Watts

Nathan Watts
Richard Watts
Thomas Watts
George Watson
John Watson
Robert Watson
Samuel Watson
William Watson
Amos Way...later Lt. in another Regt.
Samuel Way
William Way
William Weathersbee
Thomas Weathersbee
William Wayne
Aaron Weaver
Hartwell Weaver
Henry Webb
Jesse Webb
John Webb
Nathaniel Webber
Jonathan Welch
William Welch
John Wells
Thomas Wells
John Wesberry...also Westberry
Leonard West
William West
David Westcote
Robert Westfield
Plowden Weston
William Weston
Henry Watson...likely Whetstone
John Whetstone
Benjamin Wheeler
John Wheeler
William Wheeler

Richard Whitaker
William Whitaker
William Whitaker
Benjamin White
Alexander White
Andrew White
Blake Leay White
Edward White
George White
Henry White
Hugh White
James White
Joseph White
Stephen White
Thomas White
William White
Daniel Whitehead
George Whitehead
Hugh Whitesides
Benjamin Whitfield
Ambrose Whitten
Phillip Whitten
Barnet Whittington
Francis Whittington
Levi Whittington
Nathaniel Whittington
Richard Whittington
Thomas Whitfield
George Whitmore
George Wiggins
William Wiggins
Abel Wilds
Jesse Wilds
John Wilds
Samuel Wilds
James Wilkins

Samuel Wilkins
James Wilkinson
Thomas Willingham
William Willingham
Absolom Williams
Burgess Williams...also Burgis
Carroll Williams
Burns Williams
David Williams
Daniel Williams
Isaac Williams
Jacob Williams
William Williams
Henry Williams
Nemberance Williams
Nathan Williams
Phillip Williams
Thomas Williams
Jeremiah Williams
John Williams
Robert Williams
Samuel Williams
Adam Williamson
Andrew Williamson
Henry Williamson
Jesse Williamson
James Williamson
Samuel Williamson
Shadrack Williamson
Sterling Williamson
Stephen Williamson
William Williamson
Willis Williamson
Charles Wilson
Henry Wilson
Hugh Wilson

Humphrey Wilson
James Wilson
Roger Wilson
Robert Wilson
Russell Wilson
Samuel Wilson
William Wilson
Edward Wingate
Joseph Willson
John Winn
Peter Winn
Richard Winn
James Wise
Jonathan Wise
John Wise
William Wise
Gavin Witherspoon
James Witherspoon
John Witherspoon
Alexander Wood
Alexander Wood, Jr.
Benjamin Wood
Henry Wood
John Wood
Nathaniel Wood
Samuel Wood
Thomas Wood
Wiilliam Wood
Thomas Woodard
John Woodberry
Robert Woodcock
John Workman
Amos Wright
Gillis Wright
John Wright
Joseph Wright

Solomon Wright
Francis Wylie
James Wylie
John Wylie I
John Wylie II...as John Wyly
Peter Wylie
Samuel Wylie
William Wylie
Jesse Wyndham
William Wyndham
Ambrose Yarborough
George Yarborough
Own Yarborough(Owen)
William Yates
Adam Young
James Young
John Young
Matthew Young
Robert Young
Samuel Young
Thomas Young
William Young
David Youngblood

About the Author

I am a retired clinical counselor. A mother of two, a son, Richard Dunahoe, and a daughter, Eves Hayes. They, along with my Christian walk, are the joy of my life. I love being a people person. I also love reading, researching history, gardening and also being involved in my community.